SURVIVAL INVESTING

HOW TO PROSPER AMID THIEVING BANKS AND CORRUPT GOVERNMENTS

JOHN R. TALBOTT

palgrave
macmillan

SURVIVAL INVESTING
Copyright © John R. Talbott, 2012.
All rights reserved.

First published in 2012 by PALGRAVE MACMILLAN® in the United
States—a division of St. Martin's Press LLC, 175 Fifth Avenue, New
York, NY 10010.

Where this book is distributed in the UK, Europe and the rest of
the world, this is by Palgrave Macmillan, a division of Macmillan
Publishers Limited, registered in England, company number
785998, of Houndmills, Basingstoke, Hampshire RG21 6XS.

Palgrave Macmillan is the global academic imprint of the above
companies and has companies and representatives throughout the
world.

Palgrave® and Macmillan® are registered trademarks in the
United States, the United Kingdom, Europe and other countries.

ISBN 978-0-230-34122-7

Library of Congress Cataloging-in-Publication Data

Talbott, John R., 1955–
    Survival investing : how to prosper amid thieving banks and
corrupt governments / John R. Talbott.
        pages   cm
    Includes index.
    ISBN 978–0–230–34122–7 (hardback)
    1. Investments. 2. Financial crises. 3. Corruption. I. Title.
HG4521.T2834   2012
332.6—dc23
                                                        2011050317

A catalogue record of the book is available from the British Library.

Design by Letra Libre, Inc.

First edition: June 2012

10 9 8 7 6 5 4 3 2 1

Printed in the United States of America.

CONTENTS

For Alex—who always believed in his heart that the meaning and purpose of life could be found in helping others. Thank you for your friendship and support over the years. I think of you as a co-author of this book.

PREFACE

I wake each morning to a world that feels progressively more surreal, and I wonder how this can be the same America I grew up in. Every day there are new announcements of unethical behavior by bankers and politicians, and every day it goes unpunished. I'm talking about thousands of incidents over decades that have ended up costing Americans—and people around the world—jobs, incomes, and life savings.

In the interest of full disclosure, I must say I was once an investment banker at Goldman Sachs. It's funny because getting the job was one of the proudest moments of my life. Goldman Sachs in the 1980s had established itself as the premier investment bank in the world. Investment bankers were regarded as some of the brightest, most hardworking, and most dedicated people in business. Now when I am asked for a short bio, I often leave out mention of Goldman Sachs. I find it stereotypes me as supportive of a corrupt system that, in reality, I have worked much of my adult life to overturn.

Goldman Sachs was not always as it is today. We weren't saints back in the 1980s, but most of us were highly ethical people. We knew we were conducting business, not God's work. We were seeking profitable transactions, but we understood that we had clients who were issuing securities and clients who were investing in those securities, and both had to be happy with each transaction. And we understood that our reputation was everything, and that if we didn't keep our clients happy on both sides of a transaction, we risked damage to our franchise.

We had a trading operation at the time and the beginnings of a principal investment business in which we invested our own money, but they were relatively small compared with our investment banking division, which provided advice to corporations about public offerings of securities and mergers.

Two big changes occurred over time. The first was that the firm went public and began to play with other people's money. When the firm was a private partnership, it acted conservatively. This changed. Partners took out a great majority of their capital and replaced it with public monies.

I remember giving a presentation to John Weinberg, our senior partner back in the 1980s, and the management committee and telling them, "If the transaction is successful, we'll get our money back in four years." So Weinberg asked, "Why do I want my money back in four years? I've got my money now." Weinberg was so conservative with partners' capital that when we presented to him one of the first leveraged buy-outs ever completed, he refused to buy any of the equity, thinking it was enormously risky, even though the very reason to do leveraged buyouts is to create highly leveraged equity in which to invest that has enormous upside and limited down-side risk.

The second major change came when the principal-investing business and the trading business became the most important parts of the firm. Investment banking was still successful, but its profits were dwarfed by the trading business and the principal-investing business, and Goldman Sachs has always been oriented to the bottom line. And so it rewarded these trading and principal-investing partners with more senior management positions. Eventually most of the executive suite came from the trading side of the business.

The current CEO, Lloyd Blankfein, comes out of the commodities trading business, and it shows. In his testimony before Congress, he tried to present all of Goldman Sachs's business as just a matter of trades in which Goldman had no responsibility or fiduciary duty to its clients. He argued that Goldman's clients were sophisticated people, and that the firm's job was to maximize profits regardless of what it meant to the profitability of its investing clients. This is how traders think. When traders rip off clients for $1 million, whoops and cheers can be heard across the trading floor. Investment bankers spend a great deal of time trying to find loopholes in the tax laws and accounting regulations so as to maximize cash flows and reported earnings for their clients, so they are not completely without sin, but what traders do every day is much more egregious.

And there is very little value in it, other than to the trader himself. When an investment banker takes a small firm public, the banker raises capital for the firm, which creates jobs and new products and services. When a trader packages a bunch of worthless mortgages and lies to investors about their creditworthiness, he has created no value for society. The client is worse off by exactly the amount that the trader profits. It's a zero-sum game.

Academics like to argue that trading increases liquidity, thus reducing the friction, or costs, at which trades and economic transactions occur. This is partly true, but it's hardly a justification for the liberties traders take. Look at the damage done to the global economy in this latest crisis. Could all the despair of hundreds of millions across the planet possibly be worth 10 percent narrower bid-ask spreads?

So for the last 12 years, I've been writing books explaining what I think is the greatest crisis facing our country and the world—that big banks and corporations have taken over the US government with campaign contributions and lobbying. People think that banks and corporations lobby the government to get tax breaks and minor government subsidies. No, they lobby to write regulations that help them and to remove regulations that they find cumbersome. And they lobby to obtain trillions of dollars in government contracts, especially the defense industry that lobbies for unneeded weapons systems that end up doing tremendous harm in the world. The problems of the United States are myriad, yet almost all can be traced to the corporate and banking stranglehold over our government and its politicians.

In 1999, I wrote a book claiming that inequality in the United States was a serious problem that needed to be dealt with. In 2003, I wrote a book warning about the coming crash in the housing market, following it in 2004 with a book titled *Where America Went Wrong*, which warned about the dangers of corporate and banking lobbying. In 2008, my book *Obamanomics* tried to convince Obama that he would have no luck in passing effective health-care or environmental legislation, or even banking reform, until he straightened out the lobbying problem in Washington. It made no sense to me that Congress and the president would allow health-care legislation to be written by the very hospital corporations, HMO insurance companies, and pharmaceutical companies that were supposed to be regulated by that legislation. Certainly it was not in those firms' interests to see health-care costs contained in the country, and that was supposed to be the prime objective of health-care reform.

In 2009, I wrote a book titled *Contagion*, in which I predicted that our subprime problems would migrate to prime mortgages, to other asset markets, and eventually to Europe and other countries of the world.

I can't tell you why all this was so obvious to me. I had a big advantage because I was trained in sophisticated finance and so understood complex subjects like credit default swaps and collateralized debt obligations, but I couldn't believe only a few of us were sounding the alarm. What I found most discouraging was that throughout the crisis, bankers and their representatives continued to lie and steal, and academics and television pundits provided cover for them. It was as if everybody was participating in the scam and wasn't about to kill the golden goose.

Today the major argument between Democrats and Republicans seems to be who is most responsible for the current crisis, bankers or the government. Bankers are eager to point fingers at the government, saying that the government forced them to buy subprime mortgages. What people forget is that bankers and big corporations control the government. The government did pass legislation pressing mortgage originators to increase homeownership among minorities and lower middle-class Americans because these very same mortgage originators and Fannie Mae and Freddie Mac prodded the government to do that. Why? Because that is where the profits were. During the peak years of the housing bubble, mortgage originators made ten times more money on a subprime mortgage as they did on a traditional prime mortgage.

And to those conservatives who like to blame Fannie Mae and Freddie Mac for the crisis, thinking that they are agencies of the US government, nothing could be further from the truth. Fannie Mae and Freddie Mac are private enterprises with some limited implied government guarantees. They have private shareholders and managements with enormous stock option plans tied to a public stock price. And these managements took out hundreds of millions of dollars in bonuses and stock option awards during the boom. This private market incentive of Fannie Mae and Freddie Mac was what got them in trouble, not their responsibilities to the government. As a matter of fact, Fannie Mae and Freddie Mac were the biggest lobbyists of the government during this period.

Our era will go down in history as the era of the corporation. The true colonizers of today are not countries but corporations. Corporations are investing in developing countries to make arrangements with dictatorial leaders to keep wages low, prevent union formation, and keep environmental regulations a pipe dream.

Of course this conspiracy among government, banks, and big corporations could not occur without the traditional media's involvement. Journalists may be largely liberal in their politics, but I can assure you their bosses are not and their owners are not. Traditional media corporations are themselves big lobbyists, fighting for increased media concentration in big markets and dependent on corporate and banking sponsors as their major advertisers, so they're reluctant to say anything negative about either.

Although I live 3,000 miles from Washington and New York, I have been able to predict major economic crises over the past 12 years. That fact alone tells me the world is not the fair game my business school professors told me it was. It really is rigged. If it were fair, it would be virtually impossible to predict the future.

And if you aren't in on the game, it seems silly to me that you would invest your dollars in it. I think everyone in the capital markets is cheating through market manipulation, insider trading, high-speed trading, and whatever else it is that hedge funds do behind their thick walls. And investors like you are losing out.

So I write this book today in that spirit. It is another warning for Americans and investors around the world that the game is rigged and they are being taken advantage of. By investing in traditional financial securities like stocks and bonds and Treasury bonds and money market funds, they're doing nothing but propagating a system that causes guaranteed losses to investors and guarantees regular enormous paychecks to bankers and their associates.

My hope is that you come to understand that we live in a dangerous and turbulent world. I hope you carefully read this book and figure out ways to protect your family and your assets in the future.

This financial crisis didn't have to happen. It wasn't intentional, but it was a direct result of removing regulation on these banks around the world. No one likes to be overly regulated, but banks need some level of regulation. Without it they end up doing stupid things with their own debt to capital leverage ratio, their lending portfolio, and their shareholders' capital.

I'd like to thank all the people at Palgrave Macmillan, especially Emily Carleton, who have been supportive of my efforts in writing this book. Few publishing houses out there are interested in hearing criticism of our biggest banks and corporations. Palgrave Macmillan is to be applauded for its unending search for the truth and its courage in publishing the work of a small author who seeks to fight the system.

I'd also like to thank Becky, who was instrumental in typing and proofreading the book. And I'd like to thank my friends, who have always gotten me through tough times by talking me down off the ledge whenever pressures got to be too much. Specifically I'd like to thank Dottie, Lyle, and Tiki for their friendship and support during the writing of this book.

I hope you enjoy the book. I hope it motivates you to move your assets in safer directions. I hope we as a people come together and take our country back. These corrupt bankers and politicians care about nothing but their own profits and ambitions and will destroy our country and the world if given the chance to profit just one dollar more.

INTRODUCTION

When I am not writing books, I advise individuals and families about their financial decisions and asset allocation. You can see the business at my website, www.stopthelying.com. I try to keep my monthly fees reasonable because I want to attract mostly middle-income people who historically have not received high-quality investment advice from Wall Street.

My greatest selling point is that my advice is unbiased. When I tell people how they might want to allocate their assets or whether it is the right time to buy a house, they can rest assured that I have only their interests at heart. Unlike traditional brokers, who might be unloading their firm's inventory of worthless securities, I have no dog in the hunt.

I have learned a tremendous amount from my relationships with my clients. I have come to appreciate the difficult position many Americans find themselves in today. This book is a direct result of those lessons.

This recession and global financial crisis have been enormously cruel to many investors, especially those nearing retirement age. Many have seen their retirement savings decimated; they also had planned to use the equity in their home to fund a portion of their retirement. Now in many cases that equity has evaporated.

People are going to have to be wise with their future investments in order to afford a comfortable retirement, and young people need to avoid foolish mistakes in the future if they are to survive these turbulent times.

My clients are emphatically not looking to hit a home run. They just want their money to be safe. This has become increasingly difficult with the large number of defaults on the horizon, in both banking and sovereign credit, and the high risk of inflation worldwide.

What strikes me most about my clients' investment portfolios is that they hold traditional financial securities and investments as the predominant vehicles. Some held only stocks and bonds and thought that they were managing risk by moving to a greater percentage of bonds during troubled times and selling some of their stock positions. This is the standard advice, but it makes no sense. The only security I know that performs worse than common stocks during periods of high inflation is fixed-income bonds.

It is also common, as people get nervous in troubled times, to move some of their monies into what they think are cash securities. Wall Street promotes money market funds as the equivalent of cash. But if you read the fine print in a money market prospectus, you'll see that money market funds can hold lots of complex securities that are not like cash at all. They can be extremely difficult to monetize in troubled times, and they can lose a great percentage of their principal. For this reason, during the economic crisis in 2008, some money market funds started to trade at less than 100 cents on the dollar; this is also the reason that the US government came in and guaranteed all money market funds.

The competition for ever-higher yields in the money market business became so cutthroat during the crisis that many firms were taking the securities they held in their clients' portfolios and lending them out each night, then taking the proceeds and investing them in mortgage securities. Is this what you signed up for when you thought you were holding cash in a money market fund?

Holding Treasury bonds also is typical because clients think these are the safest and most secure investment in the world. I will talk at great depth about how little sense it makes to lend any country money and the troubles the United States soon will be facing that make an investment in US Treasury securities quite risky.

Of course the entire financial system is set up such that you really have few alternatives. You have to play their game. People assume you have to invest in financial securities.

The purpose of this book is to try to convince you to move monies away from financial assets and financial securities and invest more in hard assets like gold and houses and apartment buildings. The reasons are simple. I don't trust Wall Street and its complex financial securities anymore. Also, most financial securities—including corporate bonds, Treasury bonds, and stocks—do poorly in a world of unanticipated increases in inflation, whereas hard assets like real estate and gold retain their purchasing power during periods of unexpected inflation.

I spend some time in this book summarizing how bad things are in the world, but you probably don't want to hear it. As a matter of fact, you're probably quite tired of hearing how bad things are. Everybody knows it's raining. What you need is an umbrella. I want to spend a significant portion of this book describing how you can protect yourself and your family by giving you concrete solutions and real investment advice about where you might put your money to weather the coming storm. If I scare you, that is my intention because unless you are properly scared, you probably won't take any real action.

Modern life is complicated. Everybody faces personal challenges. My family has faced the same problems as everyone else: sickness, the breakup of relationships, and the loss of friends and family members.

That is why I hate the current crisis. It is a product of Wall Street, and it burdens working families around the world. Life is complicated enough without bankers and politicians piling on. It is such a large and unnecessary burden to carry.

What I want is to help people put their financial houses in order so they can focus on more important things. It never made sense to me that young couples would go into debt to pay for college and then immediately take on a half-million-dollar mortgage to buy a home. Such a large mortgage relative to their income meant they were paying almost every available dollar they earned to their mortgagor. No money was left for taking vacations, spending time with friends and family, or starting a business. It was as if they had sold themselves into slavery.

Similarly, if you're not careful, the constant volatility of the market can force you to spend an inordinate amount of time worrying about your financial position. I would like to see each of you invest so wisely that investing does not consume your life and create unnecessary anxiety for you and your family.

It is completely unnatural to watch your portfolio gyrate on your computer screen at work during the day or to come home and watch hours of CNBC television pundits tell you worthless information about how they think the market will move in the future, and it is completely unproductive. One advantage of moving into real assets rather than holding financial securities is that the time you spend managing these real estate properties and other real assets will be productive time, and you should be rewarded as a result. Almost any time you spend analyzing the earnings and growth prospects of a Fortune 500 company is a waste because hundreds of people with more sophisticated tools and better information have already thoroughly analyzed these stocks.

I'll never be popular with day traders, as I have little to say about which individual stocks to hold or how many minutes to hold them, and I certainly have no inside information. I want people to take a much longer perspective with regard to their investment portfolio, without settling for the traditional advice of buying and holding forever or of diversifying to the point of total passivity. I believe investors have to be active. It is essential not only for the health of their returns but for the efficiency of the capital market and the success of the economy.

People have asked me, given my previous accurate predictions of the dot.com crash, housing crash, banking crisis, and length and depth of the great recession, whether I'm a pessimist. I answer that I am a realist: If the world started acting and looking better, I would write more optimistic books. I feel that people around the world are searching for some means of protecting themselves from the coming onslaught, and I want to give proactive and helpful advice about how they might do this.

Although I am dealing with enormously complex financial products and terms, I am careful to define almost all terms in lay language. I understand that many very bright people have not taken the time that I have to fully understand the financial system and the complex financial products it offers. That is why they are such easy targets for financial brokers and Wall Street middlemen, but they need not be. With a little bit of work, you can become sophisticated enough to position your portfolio to generate fair returns, protect your capital, and ensure a secure future for your family.

I hope you find this book helpful. I hate people in powerful positions who use their power to lie, cheat, and steal—to profit from those less advantaged. I honestly get great enjoyment from helping people avoid the pitfalls of investing in today's world. Some day I hope to join others in bringing change to this world because I don't believe most Americans and other people of the world want to live in such a corrupt and deceitful place, but that is a subject for another book.

ONE

A DAY AT
THE RACES

My family has lived in Kentucky for more than 230 years. On my mother's side, Colonel John Steele was rewarded for his brave fighting in the Revolutionary War with a land grant on the Kentucky River. More senior officers were given land in the more desirable Virginia, and Steele found himself surrounded by woods and Indians on the Kentucky frontier.

Nearly two and a half centuries later, I found myself retracing Steele's steps as I cut my way through the Kentucky forest in an attempt to find the stone house that he built. While I never located the house, I did find a cemetery with tombstones for his daughters. This land remains essentially rugged today, and it is incredible to me that someone back then could build not only a stone house in the middle of the forest but a three-mile road to get to it and survive by shooting whatever he needed for dinner.

Kentucky, of course, is famous for four things. My parents' hometowns of Bardstown and Lawrenceburg are famous for Kentucky bourbon. Although other states may disagree, Kentucky claims some of the most beautiful women in the world. And until recently, Kentucky was famed for its rich tobacco. Now, taxes on tobacco and government payments to tobacco farmers to plant other crops have forced tobacco farmers in Kentucky to find other sources of income. Always industrious, Kentucky farmers have turned to an even bigger cash crop, marijuana.

But Kentucky probably is most famous for its fast horses. No one is quite sure why Kentucky's horses are so fast; usually the bluegrass and the limestone water get the credit. Most likely the initial breeding stock was superior, and breeders benefit from this great start even today. Much of the speed and endurance of thoroughbred racehorses rests in their breeding.

Because this book is about investing in corrupt and crooked markets, you might suppose that I'm going to tell you that I believe horse racing is a rigged game. I am sure individual races are rigged at some small tracks across the country, and certain jockeys and trainers are corrupt. But that is not my experience from watching horse races at Churchill Downs, Keeneland,

Saratoga, Belmont, Santa Anita, Hollywood Park, and Del Mar. Far from it. In fact, horse races are a wonderful introduction for anyone studying how markets are supposed to operate.

Academic papers have been written on the market efficiency of horse-racing tracks and markets. Market efficiency basically says that all publicly available information relative to how a security, or a horse for that matter, should be valued has already been incorporated in its price so it is very difficult to use public information to beat the market. For horse racing, this means that the posted odds of winning at race time reflect the best publicly available information on the probability that each horse might win.

When I was younger, I did my own small research project. I wanted to see whether the exacta payoffs for a particular race at Churchill Downs were properly priced. An exacta is nothing more than accurately predicting the horses that will come in first and second. To win you need to do both. So the odds posted just before the start of a race for each possible exacta combination should reflect the odds that any two horses will come in first and second. This is not that difficult to check, except that for a 12-horse race there are 12 times 11, or 132 different combinations of exactas that might occur. Thus, before each race, the television screen in the clubhouse shows 132 exacta prices. Also, while the odds that a horse will come in first are easily calculated from the win pool, it is a little more difficult to calculate the odds that a horse will come in second because the place pool is a bet that a horse will come in *either first or second.*

Therefore, the informed bettor must examine the place-pool odds to figure out the probability that a horse will come in first or second, then subtract the odds that the horse will come in first to arrive at the odds of its coming in second. If I then take this probability and multiply it by the probability that another horse will place first, I should arrive at the odds reflected in the exacta pool for that combination of horses. Simply put, the probability of one horse's winning multiplied by the probability that a second horse will place second should equal the payoff on the exacta.

So I did this calculation. I did it for a ten-horse race. So I had to do 90 calculations for 90 different exacta prices. Amazingly, the exacta prices that I determined were fair, based on the odds of the horses coming in first or second, almost exactly reflected the exacta odds that Churchill Downs was giving on its television screens before the race. There was a very small margin of error—say, 2 to 5 percent. To arrive at the correct probabilities, of course, I had to subtract the margin taken by Churchill Downs, which was 18.5 percent for win-and-place bets and 25 percent for exacta bets.

As a young investment banker just starting his career on Wall Street, I found this all a little incredible. Here was a small race of relatively unknown horses on a weekday at a half-filled track in Kentucky. Determining the correct payouts for exacta bets required more than 90 calculations of various odds—and this was just one race. Yet somebody somewhere in those stands was doing exactly those calculations and arriving at almost exactly the right odds for each exacta bet. I thought this was a wonderful demonstration of market efficiency. It made me wonder why anyone would bother trying to beat the stock market, which is a large, sophisticated, and well-financed market dominated by professionals, when this small horserace market in Kentucky was nearly perfectly efficient.

This idea—that markets are efficient, that it is impossible to beat the market, that the market incorporates all the best available information—is something that I was taught in business school. It doesn't mean that some people can't get lucky and generate returns in excess of the market return in the short run. But, on average, across all investors, it should be difficult to generate abnormal returns.

If the stock market is truly efficient, it also means there shouldn't be wild and unpredictable swings in market prices. While nothing explicitly prohibits volatility, if markets are perfectly efficient, dramatic swings in price must mean that new information is arriving in the marketplace. This is because efficient markets presume that a stock price already incorporates all publicly available historical information. Therefore, any big, instantaneous change in the value of a company must be the result of dramatic new information about its growth prospects or profitability.

But that certainly doesn't seem to be the case in today's market. Today's market for houses, bank shares, European debt, and virtually everything else seems enormously volatile. It's hard to imagine that there is enough new information constantly arriving to justify these market swings. But there is another explanation.

It may just be that our sophisticated and large financial markets are not as free of corruption as my little horse track in Kentucky. If markets are corrupt, then the theory of efficient markets flies out the window. There is no reason to believe that corrupt markets should be efficient or that the prices should reflect all available information. Heck, prices in a corrupt market may reflect inside information or swing wildly based on someone's manipulating the price of an individual stock. In reality efficient markets presume a level of honest dealing that I have come to believe no longer exists in our largest financial markets. Hence, the subject of this book is how individual investors can best weather a market that has become corrupted by insiders, special interests, and governments.

For a quick illustration, let's see what happens to my little horse track in Kentucky when corruption enters the picture. If we can see how corruption can destroy the fair game that is horse racing in Kentucky, we can begin to understand how corruption threatens to destroy not only our largest capital markets but the entire global economy.

So imagine you're no longer at Churchill Downs, a reputable track in Kentucky, but at another track in town, the nefarious (and fictional) Devil's Park. You and the family have decided to take a portion of your life's savings and head out to Devil's Park for an afternoon of racing. Before you leave home, you turn on the television and watch a prognosticator pick his favorite horses for the day. Little do you know that this prognosticator's station receives its funding from its biggest corporate sponsor, Devil's Park. Of course, because this prognosticator is effectively controlled by Devil's Park, he strongly encourages you to bet more than you can afford on every race at the track that day. This prognosticator never saw a horse he didn't like. (Much as CNBC and its banking sponsors have never seen a stock they didn't like.)

When you arrive at the racetrack, you are greeted by four men selling tip sheets. They swear if only you had been there yesterday, you would have won a tremendous amount of money betting on their picks. On close examination, you see that their picks from yesterday, while mildly successful, involved wagering more money than they actually made. Of course, you never find out that these tip-sheet prognosticators in the parking lot of Devil's Park are paid and controlled by the management of Devil's Park. (Just like the rating agencies on Wall Street were controlled and paid by the big banks.)

You settle into your seat at Devil's Park for the first race and look up at the tote board to see the latest odds for each horse in the race. How are you supposed to know that a trainer on the back side with inside information about how well his horse is going to run is getting ready to dump an enormous bet on his horse just before the first race, dramatically influencing those odds? (Much as some hedge fund managers do.) There is no way you can compete with such inside information. But, thinking that it is all a fair game, you go to the ticket windows and buy a $50 win ticket on a horse called Fat Chance.

The whole idea of parimutuel betting at racetracks is that all bets are pooled, and after the track takes out some small percentage for itself, the winner receives the remainder of the pool. But what if the track were taking a greater percentage— instead of 18.5 percent, as much as 30 percent of each pool? (Just like investment banks that were charging larger commissions and bigger bid-ask spreads than reported.) Bankers on Wall Street have tried to do just this through numerous means, including churning and burning clients' accounts to maximize commissions, as well as paying soft commissions to clients who direct trades their way. Today, Wall Street bankers favor exotic derivatives and mortgage securities because they are traded over the counter, off the exchange, and it is difficult to calculate how much the bank is keeping for itself.

Or what if, rather than printing just the 100 tickets that were bought on Fat Chance to win, the track printed an additional 30 win tickets and kept them for itself? (Not unlike the Federal Reserve, which supposedly controls the supply of money yet prints additional currency for its needs.) These extra winning tickets would dilute your winnings if Fat Chance did come through, yet they would never show up as part of the official winning-ticket count. It is an old scam made famous in the movie *The Producers,* when Max Bialystock sells more than 100 percent equity interest in a theater production titled *Springtime for Hitler,* in the hope that the production would be a disaster and none of the equity investors would demand their money back. Unfortunately for Max, *Springtime for Hitler* becomes an enormous hit, and his scam is uncovered because he has no money to pay all his investors.

You finally settle in your seat to watch the race, and the horses are off. All seems to be going well, and you know that if a jockey tries to throw the race near the finish line, everyone at Devil's Park will see it. But as you watch the horses on the backstretch through your binoculars, you see an unusual phenomenon. The jockeys on the three favorites in the race are pulling on the reins, forcing their mounts way to the back of the field. As the horses turn for home, the second-tier horses have such a large lead that even when the favorites are allowed to run, they have no chance of catching the field. None of the three favorites finishes in the top three, so the one-dollar trifecta—a bet naming the top three finishers in order—pays more than $16,000. You ask yourself what idiot would have made a trifecta bet that did not include any of the three favorites. But then you notice the jockeys on the three favorites are slapping high fives and laughing as they leave the racetrack. This is a classic example of market manipulation. Investors, as well as bettors at a racetrack, expect other participants to act independently, especially insiders such as the jockeys in a horse race. To the extent that some people are colluding to prevent horses from running or stocks from appreciating, they can steal enormous amounts of money from the unsuspecting public.

Let's say somehow you get lucky and Fat Chance wins the race. You go to the betting windows to collect, but you are told that, because of unforeseen circumstances, Devil's Park Racetrack is no longer solvent and cannot pay off your bet. You tear up your winning ticket in frustration. Then on the ride home, you find out that even though Devil's Park is insolvent (like our biggest banks), it is being bailed out by the federal government and has paid off all the biggest winners that day, ignoring the smaller bettors. The racetrack survived, its biggest creditors survived (like the commercial banks' creditors), but small bettors (homeowners and consumers) got the shaft.

Irate, you sit down and write a letter to your member of Congress to complain about the funny business at Devil's Park. In reply you receive a form letter from your representative, but that is all. As it turns out, Devil's Park has been paying your member of Congress $2 million a year to cover his campaign expenses. You contact the racing commission (as any investor might contact the Securities and Exchange

Commission or the Justice Department) to file a complaint against Devil's Park, but the current chair of the racing commission discourages you from doing so. You learn that the racing commission chair was once the chief financial officer of Devil's Park, and the in-house counsel for the racing commission has announced he is going to work for Devil's Park's principal law firm.

While Devil's Park, thankfully, is not a real place, the abuses I have suggested are unfortunately real in our capital markets. I will go into much more detail about how these abuses and corruptions have been allowed to occur. More important, I will examine how investors can protect themselves and their investments from the debilitating effects of corruption.

TWO

CORRUPTION
IN THE BANKS

The basic premise of this book is that global banks and world governments have been corrupted and are lying, cheating, and stealing from people. Many of you likely believe this by now, yet you continue to make traditional investments that will perform poorly in this corrupted and troubled environment.

The big question is, if the banks are so corrupt, why haven't senior bankers and banking executives been arrested? The answer is fourfold.

First, they write the rules. It is difficult to violate a law if you are the person writing the laws. We all learned in civics class (at least, those of us old enough to have taken a civics class) that Congress writes the rules and legislation in our country, but in a lobbyist-dominated environment, where the financial industry is the biggest lobbyist by far, this is no longer true. Much of the reason for this financial crisis is that bank lobbyists were successful in removing from the books important legislation that had been constraining their behavior since the Great Depression. The most famous of these is the Glass-Steagall Act, which prohibited banks from both taking deposits and conducting principal investing and investment-banking activities.

But other laws were also weakened or removed. There was a proposal in 2000 that the derivatives business, specifically the credit default swap (CDS) market, not be regulated. And in 2004, Hank Paulson, as CEO of Goldman Sachs (two years later he became US Treasury secretary), was instrumental in making sure that capital requirements for banks were loosened so that banks could leverage themselves up with debt tremendously.

During the crisis, every action taken by Paulson, who ran the Treasury until the end of George W. Bush's term, or Ben Bernanke (head of the Federal Reserve since February 2006), or Timothy Geithner (Barack Obama's Treasury secretary and former head of the Federal Reserve Bank of New York) had the immediate effect of bailing out these banks and helping them shift the true costs of the crisis from the bank creditors to the American taxpayers.

But if you're still not convinced that bankers control our legislature and actually write the rules by which we all agree to interact, you need only look at what the bankers are doing now to the reform legislation intended to prevent the next crisis. The banks are spending record amounts of lobbying dollars and campaign contributions to undo any good legislation that might have come out of the reform movement. They have delayed implementation of regulation requiring more transparency in the derivatives market. They have watered down attempts to require that they hold more capital, and they are making a joke of the Volcker Rule, which requires that they divest themselves of investing activities in which they risk depositor money for their own purposes.

The second reason that no bankers have been arrested is that they act as their own police force. Not only have they convinced auditors and accountants that self-regulation is the best form of regulation, or that whistleblowers must approach the management of the companies they're reporting on before they approach the government, the bankers also have a revolving door policy with regard to the Securities and Exchange Commission (SEC) and the Department of Justice. This means that the departing heads and senior managers of these policing organizations end up, within one or two years, working for either a bank or a large private law firm that represents banks in their financial industry group. It would be career suicide to strongly police a bank and prosecute their executives if you know that in one or two years you'll be sending your resume there. And, of course, law firms are constantly soliciting the business of banks, and banks are law firms' biggest customers.

So how does the game play out? A bank does something truly egregious. Let's say it has robo-signing procedures for its foreclosures, so that foreclosure instructions are submitted to a court without proper documentation that the bank actually has a lien on the property or can secure title to the property. The bank proceeds to evict people from their homes without any proof that it has the right to do so. Through the efforts of well-intentioned journalists and others, such behavior becomes public. (Surprisingly, these tactics are rarely initially publicized or disclosed by the SEC or the Department of Justice.) Once they are uncovered, the SEC and the Department of Justice begin proceedings to see how they want to deal with the situation. Almost invariably the bank ends up settling out of court with no admission of guilt for a relatively small fine.

But think what this means. The SEC and the Department of Justice have solid evidence of criminal behavior by the bankers that could send these executives to jail for ten to 20 years. You can imagine what happens next. They hold a meeting with these banking executives and say, "Look, I'm only going to be here in government for a couple more years, and then I'll be entering private practice. So why is it in my interest to prosecute you to the fullest extent of the law? I've got enough information here to send you up the river for years.

But rather than do that, why don't we sweep it under the rug, you pay a small fine, not admit any guilt, and be done with the matter?"

In the case of the robo-signing foreclosure case, the settlement is doubly infuriating. Not only do the bankers get off with a relatively small fine, but they pay the fine by doing something they would have to do anyway: write down to market value some mortgages they already have on their books. This, of course, generates a loss but not a *new* loss. This is a loss they've already been hiding on their books for years. The regulators argue that by recognizing this loss, the banks can now give homeowners a break on the principal amount they owe to the bank. But again, this is something the bankers would have had to do anyway because one-third of Americans are now underwater on their mortgages and will certainly not continue to be current on those mortgages. So the bankers end up getting something—in this case, complete immunity on their foreclosure practices—in exchange for nothing.

The third reason that bankers are not being prosecuted is that banks are not transparent. Banks' financial statements are enormously complex (and derivatives make them even more so), but it's near impossible for a regulator, much less a journalist, to get inside the bank and ask questions about what actually is going on (this is true of all corporations, not just banks). Journalists who care—and this number is declining rapidly in the corporate-owned media environment—can try to read a bank's tea leaves by looking at the publicly reported financial results of a bank and trying to deduce what kinds of activity, illegal or legal, might be producing those results. But I can assure you, journalists are not invited to spend time inside the banks asking everyday employees how they mark assets to market or how aggressive they are in making loans or what promises they make to homeowners to get them to sign documents. The entire corporate-dominated capitalist system is nontransparent, and banks have perfected maneuvers to protect themselves from investigative eyes.

Finally—and, in the interest of full disclosure, here I must acknowledge that I am a former investment banker for Goldman Sachs—the culture of Wall Street has seen a sea change. When I worked on Wall Street in the 1980s, the big money-maker was investment banking, so investment bankers held most senior management positions, not only at our firm but at all banks on the Street. This has changed dramatically in the years since. Traders now make the majority of the profits at the world's largest banks, so traders occupy most senior management positions. Unfortunately, the trading business is a distinctly different business from the investment banking business. In investment banking, we try to bring together two parties: an issuing party who wants to sell common stock, and an investor who wants to buy it. And the investment bank makes a substantial amount of money on successful deals when these transactions close. But whether it is an initial public offering or a merger of two companies or the spinoff of a division, I would argue, real value has been created. The assets are better positioned in the hands of investors who really want to hold those assets. So both are more productive; the investment banker gets richer, but so does the world.

Contrast that with trading, which is basically a zero-sum game. Little value is added. What traders do all day is buy things the traders think are undervalued and sell things they think are overvalued—but they must sell them to someone. So for the trader to be successful, another party has to be buying overvalued things and selling undervalued things. Now, some argue that traders create liquidity in the marketplace, and that is true—but not enough to justify the enormous physical assets dedicated to trading just to make bid-ask spreads that much tighter. After all, we can now incorporate new information into a stock price in milliseconds through high-speed trading. Is all the current volatility in the marketplace and the economy worth being able to trade in milliseconds? I don't think so. Similarly, I think anybody would pay another quarter point on a stock trade if we could be rid of the weak economy and the instability in the current global financial system. The pursuit of efficiency, the ability to get in and out of a security at low cost, has gone way too far.

So what traders actually do is rip off the less informed. If I can package a bunch of defaulting, crummy, triple B mortgages and convince you that the security they back is triple

A, and I can buy them for $50 million and sell them to you for $100 million, that is a backslapping trade of the week. As a matter of fact, in the run-up to the crisis, some individual trades netted banks billions of dollars in profits.

So in this new world where traders and trading rules dominate, and the fourth reason so few bankers are headed to jail, aggrieved parties have fewer opportunities to find legal fault with how they were treated by a bank. As an investment banker, if I didn't disclose all public information about a security I was selling, I could be held liable. But in today's trading world, no one would suggest that a trader disclose all meaningful information. The very fact that a trader knows a piece of paper is worthless is the trader's "advantage" in this trading environment. Traders are not required to ask "due diligence" questions about the securities for sale on a trading desk. The trader has no fiduciary responsibility. Traders may call the person on the other end of the phone their client, but that person isn't really a client but a stooge. The question— the only question—is how fast traders are going to separate their customers from their money. A trader can either set a client up for lots of small losses or, if the opportunity arises, rip the client's eyes out and take all of the client's money at once—and it is all completely legal.

So if you, like me, believe that enormous wrong-doing is occurring in the banks on Wall Street, it's worth making a list of their most egregious offenses. Remember, some of this activity might be legal today, but that's only because the banks are writing the rules themselves. This list consists of activities that *should be* illegal—and probably were before the recent lobbying efforts of the banks.

Probably the most egregious offense, and the most costly to society, is the banks' exertion of unfair influence and control over our democracy by lobbying Congress and making campaign contributions. Not only do these actions result in a financial sector that is underregulated, but this in turn creates a highly volatile global financial system. And because the global banking system is so important to the real economy, we end up with a stock market and real economy stuck in constant, wild swings of recessions, booms, and busts.

Many industries in a capitalist society perform quite nicely without a great deal of regulation. This is not true of banking. As I will show, because banks deal in long maturity assets and liabilities, they require good regulation and legislation to ensure that they don't overpromise and underdeliver. Someone who manufactures donuts might make stupid financing and investment decisions in her business, but luckily for her competitors, she will go bankrupt quickly because of her own ineptness. This is not true in banking.

Because the assets and liabilities that banks deal with daily are 10- and 20-year assets, their mistakes are not uncovered for generations. Stupid bankers can be stupid for 15 years before their mistakes are uncovered, and during that time, smart bankers have to meet the stupid bankers' pricing and loan terms or lose their customers and go bankrupt themselves. This is the primary reason that banks must be regulated. It is also true that in today's world many banks are too big to fail, which also requires regulation because they can't be allowed to fail in the marketplace. We also know that many deposits at these financial institutions are guaranteed by the government. This means that the depositors are not policing where their funds are invested, another good argument for regulation.

But the real damage from banks' lobbying and making campaign contributions is the destruction of the democratic foundation of our government. People are not stupid. When they see that banks have so much control over our government that money counts more than votes, people do the rational thing: They stop voting. And when people lose interest in voting, a democracy has heard its death knell. You can see symptoms of it everywhere in the United States today. Issues important to corporations—such as bank regulatory rules, patent laws, and the openness of trade with foreign countries—are not only the most important items on Congress's agenda, but they push aside the items more important to the general populace, such as education, crime, drug policies, health care, the environment, and global warming issues. These problems are never solved. It isn't that Congress doesn't work; it just doesn't work for the average citizen. It is busy delivering goodies for its campaign contributors, which are mostly the largest US corporations and banks. People like to lump the unions in as a special interest, and it's true to some degree, but it's also important to understand that the annual revenues of the Fortune 500 companies dwarf, by a thousand-fold, the annual dues of all the unions combined. It isn't even close to being a fair contest.

So after destroying our democracy, which I would argue should be illegal (and I would make all lobbying by special interests illegal and prohibit campaign contributions greater than about $100), the next most egregious thing the banks do is keep dramatic amounts of debt leverage on their balance sheets. It should be impossible to maintain a bank with 35-to-1 ratio of debt to equity (meaning that for every $1 of equity on the balance sheet, there's $35 of debt). How is it possible to run a lending business with this ratio? It means that if only 3 percent of all loans go bad, the bank goes bankrupt. The bad loans wipe out all its equity. This can't be. Bankers aren't that smart. If the bankers I know see two or three loans go bad in every ten they make, how could they make 35 loans and see only one go bad? It makes no sense to me. And it does make you wonder why banks seek such high debt leverage relative to their equity capital.

Bank executives clearly are playing a different game than bank shareholders. I believe bank executives are trying to maximize their salaries by maximizing earnings per share, and the growth of earnings per share, for as long as possible, knowing full well that they can always escape with a golden parachute if they lose their shareholders' money. Bankers also benefit from knowing the government will now bail out their creditors if there's a problem. It's silly that we put trillions of dollars of taxpayer money into the banks during this latest crisis. Yes, the banks ran through their equity capital and their shareholders suffered, but the whole idea of being highly leveraged is that banks have lots of debt investors' capital to call on in times of trouble.

Maybe half of these creditors are small depositors who need protection, but the others are debt investors in banks. They have dedicated resources to invest in banks and have earned an abnormal profit each year from holding bank debt securities. Now, when the bank gets in trouble, the debt investors are supposed to suffer. Their principal should be on the line, but that is not what has happened. Instead, these debt investors have been made whole, paid off at 100 cents on the dollar in almost all the restructurings and bailouts that have occurred to date—Fannie Mae, Freddie Mac, Bear Stearns, and on and on. And yes, Fannie Mae and Freddie Mac are nothing more than very big banks.

When Ireland's prime minister made the mistake of guaranteeing all the bank debt of his country he probably was not aware that Ireland's banks had eight times more assets than Ireland had gross domestic product. The prime minister said it was the least expensive bailout in history because all he had to do was announce the guarantee and the problem would go away. Of course, it didn't. Bad loans are bad loans. The banks were insolvent. And when they had to start marking their assets to market, they saw that they had enormous losses, which then shifted to the taxpayers of Ireland. But again, the bank creditors, the debt investors in these Irish banks, got out at 100 cents on the dollar. It makes no sense.

Now Europe is trying to apply this same formula to all the countries and banks of Europe. Somehow the Europeans think there's enough money in the world to guarantee all the mistaken loans that these banks have made and to get all the creditors out whole. European governments continue to lend money to Greece even though Greece now has $200,000 in government debt on the back of every Greek family. Think about that. Two hundred thousand dollars per family. How can a Greek family with an average income of $35,000 a year pay back $200,000 of government debt? Yet all the International Monetary Fund and the European Central Bank and Germany and France want to discuss is how to make further loans to Greece so that the Greeks can make their interest payments, rather than doing the obvious thing and haircutting the creditors to Greece, paying them only pennies on the dollar for the stupid debt investments they've made in the country. Greece's recent restructuring is far from a panacea as now new Greek debt issued in the restructuring is already trading at 15 to 20 cents on the dollar.

This leads to the next egregious offense by the banks that I wish we could make illegal and probably results from many illegal arrangements between banking executives and their clients: plain old stupid lending. When banks overleverage themselves, their lending also causes other industries and countries and individuals to be overleveraged. It's easy to blame homeowners for borrowing eight times their income to buy a house, but it's not really the homeowners' fault. Whenever too much money is granted by a lender, it has to be the lender's fault. Whenever anybody hands you more money than you can afford to pay back, it's not your fault for accepting it; it's the lender's fault for lending it to you. And the bankers have made this mistake of overlending in every sector they operate in—student loans, car loans, mortgage lending, sovereign credit lending to countries, leveraged buyout lending, hedge fund lending, and corporate lending. In every area of the bank they end up lending too much money on terms that are too loose. All it takes is a slight recession or a slight decline in demand, and the banks are suddenly surprised that many loans they made cannot be repaid.

But how do you make stupid lending an illegal act? Well, it probably results from illegal acts. It's probably the case that bank executives want to extend more and more loans so that their performance looks good in the short run, and they garner bigger and bigger bonuses, not worrying about whether the loan will be repaid in the long run. Obviously bank executives have a different incentive in this regard than bank shareholders. And so I would argue something illegal probably is going on between bank shareholders and bank executives, and where that illegality is most pronounced is at the board of directors.

The board of directors is supposed to represent the shareholders, telling management how to run the bank's assets. Nothing could be further from reality, especially at a big bank. The board consists of insiders, such as the CEO and employees who work for the CEO, and outsiders who often are friends who support the CEO, regardless of the CEO's position. Bank boards act as rubber stamps for management, rather than protecting shareholders.

Numerous changes would have to be made to the law to make boards more responsive to shareholders than to management. I'd like to see all management personnel, including the CEO, removed from corporate and bank boards. The bank boards should be elected solely by shareholders and should consist totally of outsiders, and management should be invited into the boardroom only to make presentations about suggested business alternatives and then dismissed as the board decides alternative directions for the company. It sounds radical, but I think the growth rates in our country's GDP would increase by 3 or 4 percent a year because our investments would be directed toward good projects based on their potential to generate profits, and not solely on the direction preferred by a CEO and the bank's misguided management.

Another big area—in fact, $30 trillion a year—that ought to be illegal is the credit default swap (CDS) market. For those of you who don't know, the CDS market is composed of institutions, like banks, that guarantee other institutions, like corporations, that they will not lose money on their debt investments in other companies. For example, I could buy a CDS contract, or guarantee, that says I will pay you $10,000 a year for five years, and you'll assure me during those five years that IBM will not default on $10 million worth of its debt. And if it does default, you'll make me whole on any losses I might suffer as an IBM debt holder. Well, the problem with this market is obvious. There's only $8 trillion of non-financial corporate debt outstanding. So how could there be $25 to $30 trillion in CDS activity? The answer is there must be enormous speculation. The CDS market is not being used solely as a hedging tool to protect me against the risks that my investment will sour; rather it's being used to let individuals and corporations make bets about who's going to go bankrupt first.

But this is not the real danger of the CDS market. The real danger is that it violates everything capitalism is supposed to represent. In a capitalist society, not only are winners supposed to be determined by merit and their ability to create value, but losers must be identified and allowed to fail. The CDS market makes it impossible for individual firms and individual banks to fail without pulling down the entire spiderweb.

Two analogies may help you envision this problem. First, imagine you're on an airplane in, say, Dallas, and a snow problem in Chicago forces O'Hare Airport to close. We all know that airplanes travel between two destinations, just like CDS agreements are solely between two parties. But when the snow alert hits O'Hare, it isn't just the Dallas-to-Chicago flights that are delayed and canceled—many flights across the country are delayed and canceled. The enormous complexity and interconnectedness of our air travel system causes a domino effect that shuts down other airports.

This is similar to the CDS market. Even though I enter my CDS agreement with only one other party—say, Citibank—if Citibank threatens to go bankrupt, because it is a node in this network of $30 trillion worth of CDSs, it threatens every other entity in the network.

Or imagine that ships at sea were insured by other ships at sea, instead of by Lloyd's of London back on shore. So a number of very, very large ships are out in the middle of the ocean. Call them Citibank and Bank of America and Goldman Sachs and JPMorgan. Then imagine steel-linked chains running from those large ships to smaller ships and tightened so that the web of these chains extends across the ocean, preventing any small ships from sinking (or going bankrupt). But what if one of the biggest ships itself begins to sink? Not only does its own hull begin to disappear beneath the water, it also begins pulling down the ships that are tethered to it, until every ship in the ocean sinks.

This is the outrage of the CDS system. You cannot have one failure without having all fail. This is not a moral argument; this is a capitalist argument in favor of functioning markets. And those who disagree with it typically disagree because they are making enormous profits because of how the system is rigged. But any well-intentioned outsider can see the capitalist argument is persuasive, and we have to shut down the CDS market because it is an attack on the capitalist free-market system.

Many complain that the level of bankers' pay is itself an egregious offense that ought to be illegal. I don't like the idea of a government's regulating pay at a private business, but I also understand that executive pay has gotten wildly out of control, with some executives earning 800 to 1,000 times what a typical worker in the United States makes. I would argue the problem is not with the pay structure per se but, again, with the responsibilities of shareholders and boards in their supervision and control of management. That a CEO could be earning $40 million a year suggests that no other individual in the world can perform her tasks, which is difficult to believe.

A CEO has many divisions of a company and many products to oversee. She looks at summary reports, sees which divisions are performing well and which ones aren't, and then gets smart people to focus on the problems. And if the problems are unsolvable, she closes those divisions, thus improving overall profitability. Some natural genius is involved in being a top businessperson, but no one has a monopoly on these talents. The monopoly resides in the executive's control of her board, preventing its members from looking elsewhere for those talents. If you put an ad out saying you were willing to pay $40 million a year for someone good at business, with good instincts and common sense, I assure you the line would be around the block. So rather than put a cap on executive pay, we ought to focus on straightening out our corporate boards and getting shareholders more involved, not less involved, in managing their companies. Later I will discuss how the entire concept of shareholders having a diversified portfolio forces them to hold so many assets that supervision of management becomes difficult. This also needs to be addressed.

Another absolutely criminal act on behalf of the commercial banks in this country is their outright control of the Federal Reserve System. People think the regional Federal Reserve Banks are government institutions, but they're not. They are privately owned and controlled by boards of directors appointed by our nation's commercial bankers. It is a banking-controlled operation. Back when the Republic was first deciding who should control the money supply, it was argued that we should not allow politicians to control it because they would use it for political purposes and loosen it in election years just to ensure their reelection.

So instead we opted for what some call an independent Federal Reserve. But it's not completely independent. It certainly is not controlled by voters. It's controlled by the banks. And perhaps in years past the motivations of the commercial banks were better aligned with the motivations of voters. But this is no longer true. In these difficult times, banks are at loggerheads with the general population on a number of different issues. Lower interest rates benefit the banks by lowering their borrowing costs, yet the American people, especially the elderly, are punished by not being provided with an interest rate that rewards and encourages savings.

Similarly, you would think that everybody would abhor unemployment. Certainly the people do who suffer its consequences. But from the Federal Reserve's perspective, unemployment keeps inflation in check and drives wages down, thus lowering its corporate customers' labor costs and boosting the profitability of the corporations to which the banks lend money. So, in a weird way, unemployment can benefit commercial banks. To the extent that the Federal Reserve gets involved in political decision making, it would probably argue against any debt forgiveness because it would cost its bank members money, even though it would help get companies and countries and individuals out from under oppressive debt levels and get them buying again.

The banks learned this modus operandi from their credit card business. The basic credit card business is a money loser to the banks. They extend money up front for purchases, and many of their customers pay it back before any financing charges accrue. This is a no-win situation for the bank.

Banks make money when people don't pay their balances off immediately. Banks want you to get in trouble with your credit cards. They want you to be overextended. They want you to not have enough money at the end of the month to pay back the entire principal because this is where they make all their money, and the interest rates they charge are usurious. They might charge 18 percent to a customer of good credit, even though their cost of funding is between 0 and 2 percent. This is an enormous spread for any lending operation, but it gets worse from there. At the first sign of a late payment or the inability to make an interest payment, the bank jacks up the interest rate you owe on your balance from 8 percent to 29 percent or 39 percent per year. This is why credit card lending is so profitable. It is nothing but usury under a different name, and, like most financial products, the poor end up paying the majority of the fines, fees, and expenses because it is the poor who have trouble paying off their balances.

As offensive as these practices are, what is more offensive is that the banks have taken this approach to lending and applied it to mortgages in their subprime operations, and now to student loans and the rest of their lending portfolio. But they made a mistake with mortgages. They thought if they could overlend to home buyers and get home buyers in the position that they had difficulty repaying their mortgage loans, the bank would be in a position to charge enormous fines and fees and raise interest rates on unsuspecting homeowners. But this was not a simple $5,000 credit card balance. In many cases, this was a mortgage of several hundred thousand dollars or millions of dollars. And when the bank added to the balance with fines, fees, and unpaid interest, all it did was make the loan balance larger and more difficult to repay.

A homeowner who can't repay a $500,000 mortgage certainly can't repay a $1 million mortgage. So as long as the homeowner stays current and pays higher interest rates and fees and fines, the bank is better off. But what this crisis has shown is that this type of lending quickly degenerates into such large mortgage balances relative to the values of the homes and the incomes of the homeowners that it makes repayment impossible and does nothing but generate enormous loan losses to the banks.

I argue the same thing is going on in student lending today. You see it most clearly with for-profit universities, where loans are made solely because they're government guaranteed, and people are unable to make even the first interest payment, which is what happened at the height of the mortgage crisis. But, worse, students today are graduating with hundreds of thousands of dollars of debt and poor prospects for employment—a lethal combination.

I should discuss Fannie Mae and Freddie Mac here, as I believe they are much more like a private commercial bank than they are an entity of the government, but because most people think of them as government entities, I'll discuss their problems later. Suffice is to say that Fannie Mae and Freddie Mac's problems resulted not from their government supervision but from the lack thereof and because their managements acted exactly like the managements of the big banks, worried more about the value of their option packages and their salaries and bonuses than about the overall health of their lending portfolio.

So I hope I've convinced you that even though bankers are not headed to jail, it doesn't mean that there shouldn't be a long line of bankers eventually sent there. Yes, our government is broken, but you have to understand who broke it: the bankers and the lobbyists. And to the extent that they are now writing their own rules, it's ridiculous to even talk about whether they have violated the law. They wrote the laws.

Let us regain control of our democracy and our government. Let us institute laws that not only benefit people but create an environment and a strong rule of law that allows capitalism and corporations and banks to prosper but punishes those who choose to lie and cheat and steal for the suffering they cause average families across the United States and the world.

THREE

THE UNITED STATES STUMBLES AND FALLS

The problems with the US economy and political environment could easily fill an entire book. That is not the objective of this book. Rather, this is an investment primer that aims to help you make better financial decisions. For this reason, I want to examine the health of the United States and see whether it is possible to predict when and whether it will emerge from the current crisis. I also want you, the reader, to better understand the risk of holding dollar-backed securities.

It used to be easy to invest. All you needed to do was find a stock you liked, look up its annual earnings, calculate its price-to-earnings ratio, guesstimate its growth rate, and decide whether it was priced fairly relative to its growth prospects. Today things are not that simple. You cannot ignore geopolitics. In today's world, you can earn a whole bunch of American dollars, but if those dollars don't preserve their purchasing power, you really haven't generated any real return.

An old joke makes the point. A man has robbed a bank and hidden the booty, some $10 million, by burying it in a field under a rock. He is caught but refuses to yield under interrogation, and the authorities never discover the location of his windfall. He is sentenced to jail for ten years. When he gets out, he can't believe his good fortune because he's now worth $10 million. He runs to the nearest pay phone and telephones his brother to tell him the good news. When he picks up the receiver, he hears a voice say, "Please deposit $12,000 for the next three minutes." During periods of high, unexpected inflation, investors can get killed, not just with their interest payments but with the return of their principal if it does not maintain its purchasing power.

I have a friend in New York who runs a large hedge fund. He is brilliant at what he does and works extremely long hours under intense conditions. At the end of the year, the returns he has generated for his hedge fund put him in the upper 10 percent of all hedge fund managers. He has probably averaged returns of 18 to 20 percent per year, every year, for the last 15 years.

But—and this is a very big *but*—he measures his returns in dollars. He earns more and more dollars; in fact, he has 18 to 20 percent more dollars at the end of each year than at the beginning. But is he really ahead of the game? For that to be true, he must be able to purchase more with his dollars in the future than he could at the beginning of the year. In other words, inflation has to be lower than 18 to 20 percent per year for him to benefit. At the moment that is the case, but we will see in a later chapter why this may soon change—why inflation may already be upon us.

Anyway, my friend says he feels like he's running a hedge fund in the Weimar Republic. He is properly diversified. He has properly evaluated risk. He's buying low and selling high. He's working like crazy, yet at the end of the day, all he is doing is earning dollars that appear to be devaluing quickly. It is hard to see just how much the dollar has devalued by looking at the currency exchange rates because other countries are devaluing their currencies as, or more, rapidly than the dollar. But if you look at the dollar-to-gold exchange rate, or how many dollars it takes to buy an ounce of gold, the devaluation of the dollar is evident: one dollar today buys about one-fiftieth as much gold as it did just 50 years ago.

So, in this chapter, I will explore whether we've entered an environment in which the United States will act corruptly and counterfeit its own currency. The term *counterfeit* is not strictly appropriate because the government is doing the printing of the money at the Federal Reserve. But again, in any true democracy, should this be legal? Should it be legitimate for the Federal Reserve, which is owned and controlled by our commercial banks, to print money to fund bailouts of banks in order to prevent their creditors from taking a loss? It certainly sounds like the definition of *counterfeiting* to me. And if I were king, I would eliminate the Fed's ability to print money, especially for the purposes of giving it to its supporting banks.

So is the United States actually under pressure to inflate its currency? If the United States prints more currency and produces the same amount of goods and services, by definition the price of those goods and services, measured in dollars, will have to increase; there will be price inflation. And that is exactly what's happening right now. As of today, Ben Bernanke and the Federal Reserve have printed or wired to their banks an additional $2 trillion of currency or excess reserves. This has dramatically inflated the existing currency base of approximately $1 trillion. In essence, Bernanke has tripled the amount of currency and reserves outstanding. But this analysis doesn't stop there. Is the Federal Reserve going to come under even greater pressure to continue to print money in the future?

Why would the Federal Reserve print money when it knows that doing so is destabilizing to the economy and unfair to its citizens who are trying to save? Well, the obvious reason is that the country is running enormous deficits and no longer has the ability to cut spending, and it is having difficulty borrowing money to cover these deficits because it is running excessive debts. In fact, this is a perfect description not only of the United States today but also of Japan and almost every country in Europe. I'll start with the United States.

The US debt stands at approximately $14 trillion, which is almost exactly equal to our gross domestic product (GDP), which stands at $14.1 trillion. Surprisingly, ours is not the worst ratio on Earth. That record is held by Japan, which has debt equal to 230 percent of its GDP, but it also holds a large amount of foreign currency reserves at its central bank. These numbers should scare you. As a comparison, when corporations borrow debt equal to 100 percent of their revenue, they're typically very highly leveraged buyouts. And even those typically have great difficulty paying it all back.

But the government's story is different. GDP is not the government's revenues. The government's revenues are the average tax rate for the economy times the GDP. So tax revenues in the United States—federal tax revenues—might run at 15 to 20 percent of GDP or less. As a matter of fact, although the US government spends $3.5 trillion each year, it brings in only $2.1 or $2.2 trillion in tax revenues—hence, our $1.3 trillion deficit. So government revenues are not $14 trillion (the

GDP), merely $2.2 trillion. Now, when you compare the government's debt to its revenues, our debt is not 100 percent of our revenues but closer to 600 to 700 percent. This number ought to really frighten you, especially when you realize that the United States is recognized around the world as a safe place to park cash.

Finally, even government revenues don't tell the full story here. That's because, at $2.2 trillion in revenues, we're running a $1.3 trillion deficit. When analyzing how much debt a company can handle, it's important to look at its cash flow before interest and debt expense and see how much interest expense the company can afford to pay. The government is no different. Here the relevant figure is what's available to service debt after the government has paid all its required operating expenses, such as Social Security, defense, and Medicare bills. Ideally we would find a slight positive balance, which we could then leverage up and use to fund interest payments and the repayment of principal.

Unfortunately, in the case of the United States, it's just the opposite. There is no free cash flow. Even before interest expense on the existing debt, the country has an operating deficit of approximately $1 trillion a year. How can you possibly layer more debt on a country whose free cash flow is minus $1 trillion per year? To date, the only way the Treasury has been able to do it is through a Ponzi scheme in which it issues more debt to fund the current debt expenditures of interest and principal repayments. When that Ponzi scheme stops, a lot of people holding US Treasury debt are going to be very surprised.

So our current and projected debts are one reason that you should greatly fear unanticipated inflation in the future, and you need to protect your investments from it. The second reason is the large annual deficits the government is running. These deficits are what drive governments to print the money that causes inflation. If governments had no deficits, they would have no reason to print new money.

Of course, there are more ethical ways of funding deficits than printing money. While no one likes it, an obvious remedy is to increase the tax base by raising taxes. But I've never seen such a groundswell of activity against the idea of raising taxes, even on the wealthiest citizens who have benefited most from this expansion, as I see today in the United States. It's not just that Congress refuses to allow tax rates on millionaires to be raised from 36 percent to 39 percent; it can't even agree to a reasonable inheritance tax on billionaires' money after they're dead. Haven't they heard that you can't take it with you? If we taxed even half of the inheritances in the United States, we could pay off the entire US debt in 30 years.

So if we can't raise taxes, the next obvious move is to cut expenses. But our government is broken and not for the rea-son most people think. Most people think the Republicans and Democrats disagree on everything, and there is some sort of paralysis in Washington that prevents the two parties from working together to find constructive solutions to our problems.

I disagree. The way I see it, the Republicans and Democrats are in complete agreement on the most important policy decision they make, and that is to accept bribes in the form of campaign and lobbyist contributions in exchange for subsidies, tax breaks, and government contracts to their corporate and banking supporters. Neither the Democrats nor the Republicans ever met a lobbyist they didn't like. This sole problem is what paralyzes Congress and prevents meaningful reform to deal with the most pressing problem facing the country today: money in politics. What does it mean for our deficits? Regardless of what you've heard, our deficits are not being driven right now by Social Security and Medicare and salaries of public employees. No. The big expenses are the trillion dollars a year that go to the defense industry, and the hundreds of billions that go to hospital corporations, pharmaceutical companies, and HMOs under our existing health-care policies.

Corporations and banks have figured out what the average American has not: America is on the ropes. America is in danger of going bankrupt. America is circling the drain. And what are the corporations and banks doing? They're doing what every thinking person does when transacting with a near-bankrupt entity. They're looting it. They're grabbing the last dollar. In the brightness of day, they're asking for even larger tax breaks, for more offshore tax-free dollars, for more subsidies, for more price supports, for more corporate welfare, and for bigger government contracts with greater corporate fraud and corporate waste, and they're getting it. What's causing our deficits and driving us to bankruptcy? It's the corporations and banks that are looting our government and paying Congress to stand down.

Which brings me to the next problem that will cause future deficits that will prompt the government to print still more currency: the general economy of the United States. A perfect storm is brewing for the general US economy. And as the economy of the United States declines, so do the revenues that flow to its government. The fastest way to create government deficits is a recession, which not only increases government expenditures, as unemployment insurance payments must be made and people lose their health insurance, but dramatically lowers local and federal government revenues as property taxes decline, sales tax revenue declines, local income tax and federal income tax amounts decline, and even capital gains on asset appreciation decline.

What does this perfect storm look like? First, the United States has known for 50 years that it has a demographic bubble caused by the large number of children born immediately after World War II. We have watched the baby boomers age. We have watched them go to school. We've watched them consume and work hard, and we're starting to watch as they retire. Their retirement is a double-edged sword because we lose the most productive, hardest-working generation even as its members become net users of government services, especially health care.

How have we planned for this retirement of the boomers? We haven't. Individuals have done a terrible job with their personal savings. The average 401k holds less than $12,000, and the average person older than 55 years who has a 401k has less than $60,000 in it. Until recently, Americans have saved for retirement by building up equity in their homes. It was not only their cash machine, it was their retirement plan. Now, with the decline in home prices, this retirement account has been exhausted. Many Americans are shocked that they now have zero savings and are within ten years of retirement.

Well, at least they can look forward to Social Security. As my buddy, Lee Corso, says, "Not so fast, my friend." We all know that Social Security is under threat. It is unfair to blame the current deficits on Social Security because it is a long-term insurance plan, but in 20 to 40 years, it will have great difficulty funding its current levels of expenditure. The conservative solution for Social Security, as with all things, consists of getting Americans just to work longer and harder. It doesn't seem fair to me that a recession caused by greedy bankers should be cured by all Americans having to work until age 70.

No, if everyone knew that the baby-boom generation was about to retire, the government should have been saving up monies in the Social Security trust. That is what it attempted to do. As a matter of fact, the Social Security trust fund holds approximately $3 trillion to $4 trillion in US government securities. But because the trust fund holds securities issued by the US government, the US government has funded its deficits—its operating deficits from its general operating business—by borrowing from the Social Security fund and left its notes in its place. Many people will argue that these notes are the most secure and risk-free investment you can make, but that won't necessarily be true in the future.

I have been discussing how leveraged the United States already is, how its continuing deficits dramatically increase its debt exposure, and there is no guarantee that US government debt securities will be dollar good and repaid in full in 10 or 20 years in the future. No, the proper analysis is to count that $3 trillion to $4 trillion in debt held by the Social Security trust fund as an existing, outstanding debt of the United States, making the total debt of the United States $14 trillion, and to plan for a circumstance in which either the government inflates its way out of its debt or defaults on its debt so that those holdings are not guaranteed. Social Security is required to hold its savings in government securities, but think how neat it would be if the trust fund could hold gold instead. If it held gold, it might maintain its purchasing power and would not be subject to the vagaries of inflation and the possibility that the United States will default. In essence, investing the Social Security trust fund in gold would preserve its purchasing power, just as a good investor would.

It's bad enough that the government and individuals did not save for this baby-boom retirement. To make matters worse, in the peak years right before their retirement, we went into this terrible housing price decline and recession. Just when the boomers needed the money the most, their home equity dramatically impacted their personal savings, and our government is slowly emerging from a recession that caused it to run up enormous debts. Instead of saving net monies for the looming costs of the baby-boom retirement, the government instead ran record debts that will continue to mount. How the government intends to fund the medical and retirement costs of the baby boom is anyone's guess.

The United States today has been compared with Japan in its "lost decade," which started in 1993, when Japan's real estate also collapsed and many of its corporations lost enormous amounts of money on speculative property investments. I agree with this analysis, but in many ways our situation is much worse than Japan's. Unlike 1993, today the whole world is in a major recession. That means the United States cannot look to other countries for assistance like Japan could. Second, the United States is entering this recession as an already highly leveraged country. Japan started off with almost no debt, and only through enormous and ineffective stimulus plans did it drive its debt up to its now-staggering level of 230 percent. Finally, as I have noted, the United States already was running huge deficits before the first baby boomer retired.

So the US government has put itself in an impossible position. It will find it increasingly difficult to borrow more to fund its future deficits. It is facing enormous political pressure not to raise taxes, and cutting expenses will mean closing loopholes or cutting government contracts to some of its biggest campaign contributors, US corporations and banks.

There's no simple way out. If you cut spending in a recession, you do, at least in the short run, make unemployment higher and the recession worse, meaning government revenues decline even further and deficits grow. Not that I'm a believer in government stimulus plans, especially those funded with additional government debt. I do believe that a government out of balance—spending much more than it takes in— needs to cut spending and raise taxes even though doing so will harm the economy in the short term. The important point is to minimize future pain.

The only way out—and it's not a good avenue—is to print money. The good news is that through the printing of money, inflation will reignite, the dollar will devalue, and the debt burden on corporations, banks, governments, and citizens will ease. People and institutions in debt will still have to honor their commitments, but they will be able to pay back those commitments in greatly devalued dollars. If you know inflation is going to reignite, you want to be a debtor not a creditor.

The purpose of this book is to teach investors how to deal with inflation. In this environment, stockbrokers and financial advisers are all saying the same tired thing: Put your money into traditional investments like stocks and bonds and municipal tax-free bonds and Treasury securities. What they don't tell you is that each of these securities does poorly in a period of unanticipated future inflation. You would be wise, in determining your investment philosophy, not to worry if you earn 3 percent on your portfolio while your neighbor earns 4 percent. If you can protect the purchasing power of your principal and the monies that are returned to you at the maturity of your investment horizon, you will be years ahead of the game. Investors who fight for slightly higher yields without regard for how their principal is doing relative to inflation will end up being penny wise and pound foolish. They might make an additional 50 or 100 basis points of return per year and then end up losing 50 percent of their purchasing power on their entire investment account. This book is the tool by which you can avoid that fate.

FOUR

THE ENTIRE WORLD FACES DEFAULT

The natural reaction of investors, when they find out that the United States is facing turbulent times, is to look to other countries and other currencies. Unfortunately, after you read this chapter, I think you will agree that the other countries of the world are in just as much trouble as, if not more than, the United States. The size of this problem is mind boggling. How could every advanced country of the world become so terribly overleveraged without anyone sounding an alarm? I fear that, as with the mortgage and housing crisis, so many people were making so much money off leveraging that nobody wanted to speak up.

I wrote an article for the *Huffington Post* recently in which I predicted the next financial crisis also will be global and will be ten times bigger than the subprime crisis of 2007. My economist friends immediately jumped on me, asking how any crisis could be worse than what we've been going through. I pointed out that approximately $3.3 trillion in subprime mortgage loans caused the previous crisis. We are now looking at $35 trillion in country-sovereign debt and another $12 trillion in global banking debt. If that weren't enough, economic activity in the next crisis will be severely threatened if there is no acceptable, stable currency in which to conduct business. And as I am writing this, every currency in the world is threatened, especially the currencies of the largest countries. Can you imagine trying to conduct business and trade in a world without a stable currency?

It's difficult to tell this story without sounding alarmist. The facts alone are chilling. My goal is to discuss the facts of our global financial condition objectively so that you can appreciate its severity.

You probably think the International Monetary Fund (IMF) exists to help countries that get in financial difficulty. That's what I thought until recently, when I saw the IMF leading efforts in Europe to bail out European countries and banks by making all their creditors whole. This is the same mistake

Hank Paulson and Tim Geithner made by trying to make the US bank creditors whole and Ireland made by guaranteeing all its bank debt. When the IMF organizes a debt relief package for Greece that results in a new issue of Greek debt that already is trading at 20 cents on the dollar, who is really benefiting?

I've come to the conclusion that the IMF is just another pawn in the chain of command wherein bankers control governments, and governments try to control supranational institutions like the IMF, the European Central Bank (ECB), and the European Parliament, but everyone's goal is the same: to prevent bankers from realizing losses and wealthy creditors from taking less than 100 cents on their investment dollars.

When the IMF steps into a troubled country, it does nothing more than get banks out of their bad loan positions by substituting the country's taxpayers for their underwater creditors. The IMF, through its emergency lending facilities, gives the bankers time to get out of troubled-country credits, and then, with its bailout, pays off these bankers by substituting the good faith and credit of American, French, or other country's taxpayers. It's the biggest magic act in the world. As you're watching the IMF's left hand deliver another bailout for some poor impoverished country, its right hand is reaching into your pocket and robbing you, the taxpayer, of your hard-earned dollars.

The clearest case of this is Greece. All the supposed bail-out money that went to Greece through 2011 did not reduce the amount of debt on Greece; it increased it. All it did was delay the day of reckoning, when Greece would have to default on its debt. As I mentioned earlier, Greece has US$200,000 in debt per family—but the average family income is $35,000 a year. There's no way Greece is going to be able to repay that debt, no matter how many guarantees it receives from the IMF, ECB, or anyone else. Greece is going to default, and whoever ends up holding that debt in the future is going to get back a fraction of their investment, quite possibly less than half. All the supposed bailouts have done to date is delay the process and give the banks enough time to get out of as many troubled-country credits as they can. I would bet the banks' investment advisers are pushing these sovereign credits on their unsuspecting clients worldwide while there's still time.

The numbers in Europe are staggering. The European countries of Portugal, Ireland, Italy, Greece, and Spain are the most troubled. Ireland, as I said, has eight times as many bank assets as gross domestic product (GDP). Spain's unemployment rate is north of 20 percent. For those younger than age 30, unemployment in Spain is 45 percent because all construction activity has basically ceased.

Italy's debt is already 122 percent of its GDP—highly problematic because its GDP is $2.1 trillion. Portugal, while smaller, faces a similar threat.

Conservative Americans would have you believe that Europe got in financial difficulty because of its social programs, its social democratic approach to managing its economy, and its governance. But this isn't necessarily true. Yes, European countries on average have more government spending as a percentage of their GDP than the United States, but remember, much of European education and almost all health-care expenses are provided by the state. If the health-care costs of the United States, which are now approaching approximately 15 percent of GDP, were added to our total non-health-care government spending, both federal and local, which is approximating 30 percent of GDP, the total—45 percent of GDP—would probably exceed government spending in many European countries.

No, it's not socialism that did in Europe. In fact, it's just the opposite. It's unencumbered, unregulated, completely free, libertarian-driven capitalism, especially in the financial sector. If you can believe it, the European banks are even more leveraged than the US banks, approximately 35 or 40 to 1. This means that for every dollar of equity in the company, there were $35 to $40 of depositor liabilities and debt. No bank can survive this kind of leverage. It is a real indictment of the capitalist system that, even in Europe, shareholders had so little voice and control over management. And in Europe it's not just the banks that are highly leveraged. The countries themselves have way too much debt. Greece, as I said, is overleveraged, with its debt to GDP approaching

166 percent. Again, remember, the proper ratio is not debt to GDP but debt to government revenues. So Greece has nearly four times as much debt as real government taxable revenues. Italy, we said, is at 122 percent debt to GDP. Ireland is at 109 percent. But even among the larger European countries, the United Kingdom is at 81 percent, Germany is at 83 percent, and France is at 87 percent. These are huge, huge numbers. In their excellent book *This Time Is Different: Eight Centuries of Financial Folly,* Carmen M. Reinhart and Kenneth Rogoff suggest that a country gets into trouble when its debt exceeds 60 percent of its GDP. All these countries are well beyond that.

But if you can believe it, that's just the beginning of the story. All these countries are also in a deep recession and running enormous deficits. So their debts are growing rapidly every year, and their GDPs are relatively flat. By 2017, all these countries will see their debt-to-GDP percentages increase dramatically, with Germany and France exceeding 100 percent, and the smaller, troubled European countries exceeding 150 to 200 percent debt to GDP.

And here's the worst news. These projections don't include what's going to happen to the European banks. The European banks still have not recognized the losses from the mortgage crisis, and now they face even larger losses from the sovereign debt crisis to come. They are carrying many of these troubled sovereign credits at 100 cents on the dollar on their balance sheets. This makes no sense, and the ramifications will be dramatic.

What will happen is the European banks will recognize enormous losses on their sovereign credits and their other asset positions, and technically they will become insolvent. But the countries of Europe will not allow these banks to go bankrupt. Why they don't just have the banks restructure over a weekend and pay creditors back at less than 100 cents on the dollar I don't know, but instead the countries will step in and bail out the banks at full face value. The countries will then face enormous costs because of the banks' bad lending policies. For instance, in Ireland, which has eight times more bank assets than GDP, if 20 percent of those assets turn out to be worthless, they will wipe out almost two years of GDP. If the government makes the banks whole, doing so could add another 150 percent debt to GDP to Ireland. While other countries in Europe do not have as many bank assets as Ireland relative to the size of their GDP, all of them have substantial bank assets to worry about, including Austria, Italy, Spain, France, Switzerland, and Germany.

The one country that rarely comes up in these discussions is Switzerland. Switzerland is proud of its fiscal conservatism and thinks of itself as having a stable currency, so much so that the Swiss chose not to join the eurozone but maintained the Swiss franc as their currency. All you have to know about the severity of this global crisis is that the three most desired currencies in an unstable world today are the US dollar, the Japanese yen, and the Swiss franc. I have discussed the US dollar and the US financial position. It's hard to imagine people are lending the United States money for 30 years at less than 3 percent per year. Japan has more debt as a percentage of its GDP than any country on Earth, but people seem to ignore that fact when lending the Japanese money, given that they can borrow very inexpensively and their currency continues to strengthen relative to the dollar.

The Swiss franc, in contrast, suffers from the same problem as Ireland's currency. Switzerland has five times more bank assets than GDP, and the Swiss banks were aggressive in expanding their assets during the subprime crisis and the housing and mortgage crisis, and they now hold a large percentage of sovereign credit debt. Switzerland is not that big a country. If the Swiss banks lose 20 percent of their assets to bad loans and are made whole by their government, Switzerland's debt to GDP will increase by 100 percent. Just recently, the Swiss National Bank has quadrupled the amount of currency plus bank reserves in the system, a very bad precursor for inflation of the Swiss franc. Like I say, if these are the three best currencies in the world, we all need to start buying canned goods and digging out a shelter in our basement.

So the upshot is, I can't think of a single safe country or currency in which to park your assets and investments and assure you that they won't face either default or severe devaluation as countries try to print their way and inflate their currency out of their current difficulties. This debt burden not only threatens the banks and countries of the world but is a dead weight around the neck of a global economy that refuses to recover. There can be no consumer demand when consumers are facing such enormous debts, and governments can do little to create artificial demand if their debts are at an all-time high.

It certainly looks like a conspiracy to me. I thought the same thing during the US mortgage crisis, and I was vindicated by what happened during and after the crisis, especially the deadend fate of proposed reforms to the banking and government systems.

I used to hesitate to use the loaded word *conspiracy,* but I can't think of a more apt term for a world in which banks have such power over governments. In the United States it's rather blatant, with bribes to our government officials in the form of campaign donations and lobbying expenses.

I'm not sure how bankers in other countries of the world manage to bully their governments, but it certainly happens. Bankers and ex-bankers hold all the critical positions on the finance staffs, not only in these countries' governments but in the supranational organizations like the ECB, the IMF, and the European Parliament. It may sound trite, but bankers really do run the world. Like the Fed, if a banking organization like the ECB is determining how much to inflate the euro and how much to stimulate growth and when it should be concerned about unemployment, and it works solely for the benefit of the banks and not individual citizens, what other conclusion can you draw? And this is the very direction the bailouts in Europe have taken.

First banks tried to cover up their mistakes, and that didn't work. Then governments came in and tried to bail out the banks, and that didn't work. And now supranational organizations like the ECB and the IMF are trying to figure out a way to bail out countries that bailed out the banks, and that's not going to work. It is as if these allegedly sophisticated minds think that all you have to do to ensure repayment of a debt is to find a larger entity to guarantee it. Nothing could be further from the truth. These are bad loans. This is not an optics problem; this is a real cash-flow problem. Leaders in Europe and the United States are acting like this is just a liquidity crunch, and that we'll get through it if we just get rid of the fear factor. That is irrational thinking in its purest form. People are correct to be pulling back from investing in banks and country debt because they know they're not going to be repaid. There's no cash flow.

So the problem keeps getting pushed to a higher and higher level. Countries like Germany and France aren't big enough to guarantee countries as large as Italy and Spain and all their associated debt. So now Europe is trying to pull some half-trillion dollars together to guarantee all the debt of all the banks and all the countries in Europe, but even that won't cut it. Tiny Greece, with a $300 billion economy, has already burned through $200 billion in bailout money. Certainly $500 billion isn't going to last long.

So what's the European solution? You won't believe it. They're going back to the Hank Paulson and Tim Geithner playbook. They're creating special investment vehicles (SIVs) to try to leverage this half-trillion dollars to do things off the balance sheet, just like the US banks did back in 2006. If that's not enough, they've also spoken about creating a credit default swap (CDS) market for these countries, in which the $500 billion won't be used to directly bail out these countries but rather to guarantee their debt. Well, this is exactly what AIG did and got itself in trouble because just guaranteeing a bad debt doesn't make it good. And when it finally does go bad, all these CDSs will come back to haunt these European credit providers, and of course they won't have the monies to fund all the losses that result.

Finally, and most incredibly, they're talking about a collateralized debt obligation (CDO) structure. If you remember, CDOs started all the trouble in the mortgage market. This was where a bank put all sorts of junk mortgages into a security and then layered it in tiers, where the first defaults went to the lowest tier, and the second defaults went to the middle tier. And only after everyone defaulted did the top tier face any loss of principal. But as we saw in the mortgage crisis, because all the mortgages placed in the CDO were complete junk, all three tiers of the CDO suffered enormously. Some of the top, AAA-rated slices ended up losing 92 percent of their principal.

And this is the solution that Europe has chosen. The Europeans want to take their $500 billion in real capital, leverage it up, and layer more senior debt on top of it. The $500 billion would take the first hit on country default losses, another completely stupid idea that proved to be enormously damaging in the United States during the mortgage crisis. Ever wonder what happened to all the investment banking geniuses who brought us the subprime crisis? Well, it looks like they're happily employed on the European bailout. I was shocked that these people caused this global financial crisis, but I was even more disturbed to see how little they've learned from it.

I've tried to think through a more appropriate solution for Europe's problems. I envision a chart that shows which countries owe monies to which other countries and which country banks owe monies to other country banks and to other countries. As you can imagine, it's an enormous, complex diagram. But suddenly you notice that in every case the arrows are flowing in both directions. Yes, Greek banks owe French banks money. And, yes, the Greek government owes the French government money. But surprisingly the French government also owes Greek citizens money. So if everybody is overleveraged, someone should calculate the net of everyone's exposure. In essence, I'll forgive your debt to me if you forgive my debt to you. This way you can blur the lines between countries and banks and pension funds and simply look at who is in debt to whom and to what extent. The fact of lending is that when someone defaults, there is a winner and a loser. It is a zero-sum game, not a permanent loss of global wealth. It's just a shift of wealth. And if we could restructure all these balance sheets and net out all this cumulative debt, we'd be in a much better position to restructure any remaining debt so overly burdensome as to be destructive to the growth of the global economy.

I know what you're thinking. It will never happen—it makes too much sense. And that's the world we live in today. People in power are not trying to solve problems; they're trying to cover their tracks and please their financial supporters. Bankers are trying to avoid writing off bad loans. They're trying to avoid taking losses. They're trying to preserve their earnings per share and their stock prices, and they're doing it stealthfully and without transparency. They're doing it through cheating, lying, and, in some cases, stealing. It's why I wrote this book. It's why you must protect yourselves because the powers that be, both banks and governments, are going to come looking for assets to make them whole. And I think they're going to come after yours.

FIVE

NO REFORM
COMING

I can imagine many of you are enormously frustrated at the pace of reform in the world's banks. "The pace of reform" is completely misleading because it suggests that reform is proceeding, albeit at a slow pace. Nothing could be further from the truth. No reform is actually occurring. There's a lot of paper shuffling and a lot of wrangling behind closed doors, but the discussion in the United States is among the bankers, their lobbyists and law firms, and the politicians to whose campaigns they contribute.

I wrote my first book in 1999 about what I thought was a serious but underdiscussed issue of the growing inequality in income and wealth in the United States. I had to wait 12 years before someone seriously mentioned it as an issue. The media wouldn't listen. I appeared on radio and television, but no one wanted to discuss lobbying or the undue influence on our government of special interests like banks. I sadly watched the entire financial crisis unfold with incalculable human cost in the form of unemployment, lost wages, decimated savings accounts, cracked pensions, and people thrown from their homes.

The response of our government to the financial crisis was inept. Somehow the world went crazy for a new Keynesian version of economic stimulus, and almost a trillion dollars was spent with nothing to show for it. Worse, the stimulus was financed with government borrowing the money so there could not be any positive effect to the long-term economy. Monies spent today to stimulate the economy would have to be repaid when these debts came due in the future. The thought that government could stimulate economies, create jobs, and encourage new industries flies in the face of everything history has taught us about state-run enterprises and economies.

I watched in horror as Ben Bernanke decided to print $2 trillion in new money to buy bad loans from the banks, buy mortgages in the open market, and try to stimulate the market in US Treasury securities. Of course everyone came out in favor of cutting interest rates, not realizing that the big beneficiaries were the banks—which borrowed at near-zero interest rates and lent the money back to the government at 3 to 4 percent a year. No one even mentions that our elderly, trying to get by on fixed-income-type returns, saw their savings yield less than 1 to 2 percent a year.

Was no one else shocked to see that in a world of huge government deficits, the government's response was to increase stimulus spending and to propose tax cuts? What kind of logic is this? Of course Democrats love government spending because it preserves the wages and jobs of government workers, who are one of their largest constituencies, and Republicans love tax cuts because it favors their corporate, banking, and wealthy family constituencies—but neither action does anything to reduce a deficit.

Finally, the United States and Europe arrived at the silliest conclusion of all. In a world overwhelmed with debt, the governments of the world decided what was needed was more debt. They lent more money to the banks. They lent more money to troubled countries. They even lent more money to individuals who were upside down and underwater, with their mortgages worth more than their homes.

But the most disturbing thing about this entire crisis has been watching our feeble attempts at reform. The very public attempts by Congress to pass new legislation stalled under incredible lobbying pressure from the banks. Even now much of the legislation has not been enacted; the rules cannot be written because banking lobbyists keep getting in the way. The banks' own law firms have been hired to do a great deal of the writing of the legislation. Sullivan & Cromwell—probably the Wall Street firm most closely associated with the biggest banks, as its senior chairman, Rodgin Cohen, used to be the head of Sullivan & Cromwell's financial institutions group—has written much of the legislation, and of course it's thousands of pages long so that no one knows what's in it or where the loopholes are. Gary Gensler, a former partner in Goldman Sachs and now head of the US Commodity Futures Trading Commission (CFTC), took nine months to try to write rules to make derivatives more transparent; he finally gave up and asked for another year before he publishes his rules. Let's hope we're all still here in a year.

One of the most disturbing battles has been about the question of how much capital banks should be required to hold. My good friend Anat Admati of Stanford University has spent countless, sleepless nights fighting not only the banks, their law firms, and their paid members of Congress but even our own academic community in an attempt to simply explain that if banks are financed with more equity and less debt, the financial sector will be more stable and the global economy less volatile.

In 2010, I could no longer stand the failure of Congress and the administration to tackle the serious problems and issues facing our country, and I wrote a short piece for the *Huffington Post* that listed all 47 areas that desperately needed to be addressed. I think you will find that list to be illuminating, so I will give you a summary.

1. Overleveraging of banks
2. Artificially low interest rates
3. Lobbying and money in politics
4. Too much debt everywhere
5. Depositor insurance
6. Exorbitant fees for bank consumers
7. Predatory lending
8. Global investor diversification
9. Credit default swap market
10. Criminal behavior of bankers
11. Boards of directors that ignore their fiduciary responsibilities
12. Securitization (taking a number of disparate assets or securities and bundling them into one security to be sold in the marketplace, supposedly increasing liquidity and attracting new sources of capital)
13. Toothless rating agencies
14. Fannie Mae and Freddie Mac
15. Too many financial middlemen
16. Too much overlap of regulatory bodies
17. Financial institutions that are too big to fail
18. Bank market concentration of monopoly power
19. Adjustable-rate mortgages

20. Teaser interest rates

21. Low down payments

22. Personal bankruptcy law preventing writing down mortgage values

23. Lack of regulation of long maturity asset industries

24. Excess reserves (commercial banks are required by law to hold a small percentage of their total assets with the Federal Reserve—any excess needs to be tracked and explained because high powered money, the best determinant of inflation, is composed of currency in circulation and total reserves held by the bank at the Fed)

25. Existing risk management policies at the banks

26. Few restructurings of insolvent banks

27. Lack of regulation for hedge funds

28. Management incentives better aligned with shareholders' interests

29. Complexity of mortgage and investment banking products

30. Banks' failure to recognize bad loans

31. Ineffectiveness of government stimulus

32. Weakness of new bank regulations

33. Excessive compensation for bank executives

34. Undervalued Chinese currency

35. Globalization and its effect on wages

36. No bank transparency

37. Externality costs and collective action problems

38. No accountability for Federal Reserve

39. Slow response times to crises

40. Underwater mortgages

41. Risks of Social Security and Medicare insolvency

42. Corporate ownership of media

43. Insider trading and market manipulation

44. Lack of requirements for public reporting of publicly traded corporations, hedge funds, and banks

45. Overnight market in repurchase agreements (the repo market)

46. Corruption in government

47. Collapse of global banking system

Not one of these problems has been sufficiently reformed in the intervening years. How could so many important areas be missed? You could throw darts at a dartboard and hit at least some of these items. The only way you could miss all 47 is intentionally, and that's what's going on. There's a lot of talk, but the banks still control Congress, and unfortunately all attempts at reform are being watered down by the banks and their lobbyists.

The only bright spot is the Occupy Wall Street movement. I, like other people, was a bit skeptical initially because the movement was led by artists, actors, and puppeteers. I was afraid they didn't have a firm grasp of the economic and political issues in play. Boy was I wrong. It just goes to show that you don't need an MBA to understand what is criminal about the current system. The Occupy folks finally put out a short list of demands, and they were right on. Amazingly they didn't focus on superficial things like executive pay but got right to the heart of the matter. They understood this was not just an economic problem and not just a banking problem but a geopolitical problem.

Their first demand was the reinstatement of Glass-Steagall. Second, they wanted Wall Street criminals investigated and prosecuted. Third, they wanted the Supreme Court decision in *Citizens United* reversed. This Supreme Court decision allows corporations to influence political campaigns in the form of paid advertising any time during an election. Fourth, Occupy wanted to pass the Buffett Rule on fair taxation so that the wealthy pay their fair share and corporate-tax loopholes are closed. Fifth, Occupy wanted to completely revamp the Securities and Exchange Commission. Sixth, the movement wanted to limit the influence of lobbyists and eliminate the practice of lobbyists' writing legislation for Congress. Seventh, Occupy wanted to close the revolving door that allows former government regulators to go to work for corporations and banks, and former bankers and corporate executives to work for the regulatory agencies that oversee their industries. Eighth, Occupy wanted to eliminate corporate personhood—the legal doctrine that extends the rights of and protections for people to corporations.

I don't think I could have come up with a better list myself. I've been against personhood for corporations since the beginning because there is no way you can give political rights and power to a corporate entity that by law has only one guiding principal—the maximization of shareholder value and the maximization of profits. Occupy Wall Street's main mantra is "We are the 99 percent." The movement is correct when it says that the entire lobbying and campaign contribution system allows corporations, banks, and wealthy individuals—the remaining 1 percent of the population—to control our democracy.

A narrow focus on profits works well for a corporation in the marketplace, but in the world of ideas, like a community or government, the electorate is faced with ethical and moral questions that corporations can't understand and, by their own charter, refuse to. Much of government is an attempt to solve collective action problems, an arena in which the marketplace alone, with its independent self-centered agents, has no place. Allowing corporations into politics certainly makes no sense because their self-centered behavior is exactly the reason that many collective action problems exist in the first place.

At least some things have become clear to those who have been watching this farce called the reform movement. Bankers are different from you and me. Jamie Dimon, the CEO of JPMorgan Bank, is indeed a smart man, but I've never heard a smart man say so many stupid things. He is 100 percent consumed by trying to increase the earnings per share of his bank, thinking that will increase the value of his options and his personal wealth. He does not understand the first thing about the risk that his firm is undertaking, or the damage he's doing to the global financial system and to the global economy, by being so highly leveraged and so interconnected with other financial institutions through the derivatives market. It would be laughable if it weren't so sad, given the damage he and other bankers are causing to our global economy. How someone of his intelligence can be so narrow minded is incredible to me.

We have created a generation of MBAs, and the leaders of our corporations and banks are cost-benefit experts who spend their evenings and weekends reading annual reports and company financials. They have no empathy for people who are suffering because they don't have time to meet ordinary people.

Second, it is impossible to watch the traditional media's coverage of this crisis and the reform movement without realizing that the media are not unbiased. The media are owned by corporations, and banks and corporations are their biggest advertisers.

This is the world we face. The people can battle big corporate power and big banking power but only if they have a method of communication by which to organize. And traditionally that has been the media. To take the media out of the equation makes it much more difficult for people to be properly informed, properly motivated, and properly organized. The best hope is that the Internet replaces the traditional media and does not itself become another arrow in the quiver of corporate power.

Another sad exposure during the reform movement has been the inept response of many of my dear friends in academia, at the business schools and in economics departments across the country. They have been exposed as friends of and shills for the big banks, hedge funds, derivatives industry, and big corporations. In a later chapter, I will address in more detail the shortcomings of many of our economists, not only in predicting this crisis but in reacting to it. Of the tens of thousands of economists in the world, I can count on two hands those who are actively working for real reform. It seems every article on the topic is written by one of a few people: my good friend Daron Acemoglu or Simon Johnson or William Black or Robert Reich or Anat Admati. Where are the other economists? Why are they so quiet?

I've concluded that too many of them have been bought off. Most people don't understand how top economists at our universities and business school professors are paid, but I can tell you that the biggest contributors to universities and to these professors' paychecks are the banks. Their best students at the business schools and in economics departments end up working for the banks. The professors' biggest speaking fees and consulting assignments and expert-witness fees come from the banks, so these academics are not about to criticize them. The professors' silence is deafening in a world gone crazy with tens of millions of people suffering. These experts, trained for decades in how to properly run an economy, are strangely quiet when their talents are so desperately needed.

It is interesting that of all the economists who have looked at the problems that this crisis has exposed, the ones who actually get it are the experts on developing countries, the political economy folks. They have studied poor countries around the world and understand why these countries aren't making progress: lack of good institutions, absence of democratic and voting rights, inability to press for civil rights and press freedoms, no stable currencies, no property rights, and no rule of law. Many are oligarchies in which the rich control the economy and the government, and the only people who get special favors are people who happen to be rich because of the government's largesse.

I too studied developmental economics because I wanted Argentina and Mexico to be more like the United States. Never did I imagine that, instead, the United States would become more like Argentina. We have violated every principle I learned about how to develop a successful and prosperous economy by creating an environment that is fair and just to all workers. We have created an economy, a government, and a social system in which all benefits accrue to the rich, all monopoly power to corporations, and all dollar influence to banks, and individuals and families become slaves to a corporate-dominated system.

I think, from an economic perspective, my greatest frustration is that people, even economists, still don't understand one basic principle: The banking industry is different from all other industries. Like the insurance industry, it deals in long-maturity assets and liabilities. Therefore, you cannot trust managers or board members or shareholders or even the marketplace to properly discipline aggressive management. Executives in the banking industry can do all sorts of stupid and overaggressive lending to generate bigger market share, bigger growth, and bigger profits in the short run, and cash out their bonuses and be gone before the bad loans come back to haunt the bank.

A free market is ill prepared to handle such a time lag. That is why the insurance industry—and, once upon a time, the banking industry—were highly regulated. It is also why deregulation can work in some industries. When the costs of bad behavior by management show up quickly, you don't need a great degree of governmental supervision because the market takes care of it. Those companies go bankrupt quickly. We would be in much better shape if more economists and policy makers understood that banking is not like other industries and cannot survive unregulated.

Learning this fact is crucial not only for the survival of the financial and banking industry but for the entire capitalist system because a bank's raison d'etre is to allocate capital for the system. It is its primary objective. And what I'm saying is that, if left to their own devices, banks do an extremely poor job of allocating capital efficiently in a capitalist system. That's quite an indictment, of not only the banking sector but all of capitalism.

Left to its own devices, the banking community will cause booms and crashes and busts, and probably will create zero growth and zero value. That's not the story capitalists want to tell. Capitalists ought to be fighting to strictly regulate the banking industry. The global banking industry is killing any growth in the world today. Without reform, it will kill capitalism.

I'm pessimistic. I believe we are in the midst of a great power struggle in which the rich and powerful and organized are aligned against everyone else. One side has all the money. And, to make matters worse, it has the support of the traditional media. An optimist would say that true power resides in the people, and the people united will never be defeated. Gandhi said, "All tyranny fails eventually. Think of it always." I'm not so sure. Please prove me wrong.

SIX

THE LOW-WAGE
THREAT OF CHINA
AND INDIA

G iven all the damage that the banking community has done to the global economy since the
early 1980s, it's hard to believe that another,
even more destabilizing economic force is at play in the world
today. But there is—free trade by advanced countries with
low-wage countries such as China, India, and Vietnam.

If economists learn but one thing in school, it is David
Ricardo's early nineteenth-century theory of comparative advantage. It is the basis on which almost every economist in
the world supports free and unfettered trade between nations.

Although hundreds of empirical studies have been conducted in an attempt to demonstrate that Ricardo was right—those countries that trade more are more prosperous or grow faster—none has succeeded. So the unfortunate agreement among economists that trade makes all countries better off is based without exception on their belief in David Ricardo.

Ricardo's basic premise is that if two countries have different skill sets—if Italy can make shoes faster and better than the United States, and the United States can make computers better and faster than Italy—then it makes sense for the two countries to trade, even if one of those countries can make both shoes and computers faster and better than the other and of better quality. Ricardo is saying that if you allow the country that produces one good more efficiently to focus exclusively on that good and allow the other country to focus on producing the good that it does relatively better, you will free up work hours that can be used to increase total production.

But David Ricardo never envisioned the modern world. Who would have thought that the advanced economies of the world—namely, the United States, Europe, Japan, Canada, and Australia—would employ nearly 300 million people, and yet in a few decades, India and China alone would introduce an underemployed labor supply of more than a billion adults ready to work for next to nothing? Since the early 1980s, as these two countries opened their borders, emphasized capitalism as a means of growth, and began active trading with the developed world, it has been as if somebody opened the tap and turned on a limitless supply of inexpensive labor—a capitalist's wet dream but a labor organizer's worst nightmare.

There is no denying that if China can produce a high-quality shirt for $3 and it costs $15 to produce a similar shirt of similar quality in the United States, the United States in general would benefit from buying all of its shirts from China. Certainly the people who manufacture shirts in the United States will suffer in the short run, as they will lose their jobs and have to reposition themselves in other industries, but the net effect remains positive. Instead of paying $15 for a shirt, Americans have to pay only $3, and all the people who were making $15 shirts become available to use their skills more productively in other industries. As a general rule, if you can buy $15 shirts for $3, you should buy as many as you can. And that's what we did.

But this analysis of David Ricardo's theory leaves out two critical elements. The first is that even if both countries benefit from trade, it doesn't mean that benefit is spread evenly across the population. Certainly business owners in the United States love the idea of an endless supply of inexpensive labor. They will outsource jobs to low-wage countries, and they will threaten to move plants there in order to bust unions and justify lower wages and fewer benefits for their workers. Workers in the United States and other developed countries will be less enthusiastic about their new competition.

And make no mistake. The reason that China is able to offer labor at such low wages is not because the Chinese are more efficient or more productive than American workers. It is simply because the cost of living is so much lower in China. And the reason that the cost of living is so low in China is because there's a glut of underemployed people willing to work for next to nothing. So as long as this glut of underemployed people exists, the developing world will be able to produce goods less expensively. Their cost of labor will be less, and jobs will move to those countries.

The other element that Ricardo's theory ignores is that there is a second-tier effect so important that I believe it negates the positive aspects of any wealth creation from trade. It is this: when the mass of workers, especially unskilled workers, in the developed world become unemployed or unemployable because of trade with low-wage countries, this trade destroys the middle class of the developed countries. We have seen real wages for Americans stagnate since the early 1980s. Now, in this recession, the brunt of the costs of the crisis are falling on the middle class, young people just getting out of school, and men and women older than 50 who are being pushed out the door with little chance of finding new employment. The real cost of trade with low-wage countries was hidden from most Americans for decades but is now becoming apparent in this difficult economic environment. It's not clear to me that the unemployment rate in the United States and the rest of the developed world will ever return to its historic lows. There could easily be a permanent unemployed class in these countries simply because economics dictates that all the low-skill and manufacturing work, and now some Internet-based service industries, are going to move to India, China, and other low-wage countries.

Capitalism focuses on creating economic value by creating economic profit. In its purest form, it does not address the question of job creation. It is presumed that labor is just another ingredient in the manufacturing process, and that, if priced appropriately, labor markets will eventually settle near full employment. But you can see what this huge group of underemployed people in the developing world is doing to that equation. Equilibrium cannot exist when a billion people are willing to work for next to nothing just to survive. Worse, the country with which we have increased trade most, China, is a communist dictatorship that basically prohibits free speech, labor unions, and a free press. Again, an ideal situation for a capitalist who doesn't want to see his workers organize into unions or collectively assemble to air their grievances—but not the type of world that Americans and Europeans would have hoped for.

A hard-core libertarian might argue that the market is always right, that the market determines the value of people's wages—that if people can't find employment, they have themselves to blame for not having the appropriate skills. But we know that, in advanced countries like the United States, there will always be a percentage of people who, for whatever reason, do not go to college or acquire high-tech or high value-added skills. There will always be a high school-educated working class. For the rich elite who run countries to put this working class in competition with a limitless supply of dollar-an-hour labor is beyond harsh. It is unethical and unfair.

To clarify, let me describe a different world. Let me describe a tenth planet that revolves about the sun, and on this planet everyone has one profession. Everyone is a doctor. As you can imagine, they are all highly trained, highly educated, and highly skilled, but there just isn't the need for that many doctors on this new planet. Therefore, doctors on this planet earn approximately a dollar an hour for their services, and most are unemployed.

I just have one question: Would the doctors in the United States and Europe be in favor of free trade with this planet? Would they welcome the outsourcing of medical services to doctors from this planet or allowing free emigration from this new planet to Earth to allow these underpaid and unemployed doctors to flood the US and European labor markets? I doubt it. And yet that is exactly what we did to our manufacturing and low-skilled workers. We punished the most those with the least. And the profits that resulted from hiring dollar-an-hour workers in these developing countries all went straight to the top. The top 1 percent of Americans saw their percentage of the national income double in the last 30 years. And the 400 richest Americans now have total wealth equal to the 50 percent of poorest Americans. Think of that. Four hundred people out of 310 million Americans have wealth greater than half the people in the country combined.

To get your hands around this problem, you must understand a concept even most economists fail to see. Most economists believe that the market determines wages and that whatever the market determines as your wage is a fair value for your services. Many economists believe your salary determines your worth to society. If you get paid a higher salary, you have greater value and greater worth to society. But this is simply untrue, in a world with so many unemployed people with low skills. The level of wages determined in a marketplace measures only how scarce a person's supply of services is relative to the demand for those services. In a perfect world, people would change jobs, moving from one industry to the other seeking the highest wages, and those jobs that require greater investment and greater education would always pay higher salaries, but this is not the case.

Look at the simple example of business school professors. They are some of the brightest finance minds I know. They are not underpaid; many earn more than $200,000 a year for teaching and doing their research. But their young students head off to Wall Street and within three or four years are often making millions of dollars a year. Who is creating more wealth for society, the young trader who brings in $25 million in profit for his firm and takes a $10 million cut or the business school professor who trains a hundred of these traders to do such miracles every year?

In a world now dominated by a crisis brought on by our banking community and its domination of our political environment and governments of the world, it's hard to imagine an economic force of equal or greater magnitude, but trade with low-wage countries is having a devastating impact on the advanced democracies of the world. It's not just that wages are stagnating in these developed countries. It is that the middle class is threatened, and this threatens democracy itself. I think it makes a lot more sense to slow growth in low-wage China and India by slowing their exports to the developed world through tariffs or other such arrangements so their people can still eventually grow out of poverty but not at the cost of destroying the middle class and democracy in the advanced world. Similarly, immigration to the United States and Europe can be slowed from the developing world to better protect the wage structure of our middle class. It makes no sense to me to sacrifice the advanced democracies of the world on the altar of free trade and unlimited legal and illegal immigration.

Protests in the streets of Tel Aviv, Sydney, New York, Oakland, Boston, Madrid, and Athens all have a common theme. Young people, unemployed people, and hard-working people are recognizing that 99 percent of the people do the work and 1 percent of the people reap the rewards. The system is unfair. Capitalism has failed to reward those people who actually do the work.

And the way capitalism is structured today, that shouldn't surprise you. For, you see, shareholders manage to congregate, organize, and structure themselves as a corporation and speak with one voice when hiring an individual, but more and more, because of the threat of low wages from developing countries, individuals are having trouble organizing themselves into unions to negotiate their salaries with these corporations. It's a one-sided game. Recently, the state of Wisconsin and others have considered taking away collective bargaining rights from public employees. This would mean one individual seeking a job as a janitor in Wisconsin has to negotiate on his own with the entire government of Wisconsin. What kind of justice is that?

So if trade with these low-wage countries is the primary force driving greater inequality in the advanced world, how dangerous can this movement become? The answer is very dangerous. We have seen in the United States what happens when all wealth is concentrated in a few hands. The people with the money rule. They have undue influence on Congress, the president, and the electorate through paid advertising in the media. Money talks. Or, as the Supreme Court said, "Money is speech." We like to think that everyone in a free democracy has the right to free speech, but how can we balance it if I am speaking to an audience of three and you are speaking to the president over breakfast, your congressional representative at lunch, and the entire American public through television advertising in the evening? Clearly more money buys more listeners and listeners with more clout.

And this is the danger of allowing money into politics—not just corporate and banking money but individual and family wealth. Just because you're rich, you shouldn't be able to buy more justice. And yet, of course, in our legal system, the wealthy get better lawyers and the poor go to jail.

Just because you're rich doesn't mean you should have greater access to your congressman or to $50,000 breakfasts with your president. All Americans should have equal access to their government representatives regardless of how much money they have or how connected they are. Just because you're rich doesn't mean that your ideas about an election or a referendum ought to be broadcast on the airwaves a million times more powerfully than my simple speech. The Supreme Court thinks that by allowing corporate advertising during campaigns, it is increasing the amount of speech, which it thinks is a good thing. What it fails to see is that the volume of certain people's speech is increasing, but it is drowning out the speech and views of those not able to spend millions on television advertisements.

Just because you're rich doesn't mean that you should be able to lobby the government to pay less taxes than the average American, pay capital gains rates instead of ordinary income rates if you're a hedge fund manager, and prevent the taxation of your inheritance, thus guaranteeing your children a rarified position of wealth and status not through merit but simply through birth. This is a form of the monarchy and inherited bloodlines that Americans revolted against 230 years ago in Europe. We did not want a class-based America. We did not want status based on inherited position. We wanted to establish a meritocracy, a country where people would be free to pursue their life's dreams, and everyone would have equal opportunity to do so. That is not the America we have today.

So you won't hear this from any economist because they're still basing their thinking on a flawed 200-year-old economic theory. The truth is, even the most elegant theoretical models have their limitations when applied to the practical world. We must ask ourselves what assumptions are behind the model that do not reflect the realities of today's world, and what damage can be done by simply following a recipe for disaster that a brilliant man concocted hundreds of years ago.

SEVEN

WHY ECONOMISTS DON'T GET IT

As an investor, how can you be expected to understand what's going on in the economy if even professional economists don't have a clue? This crisis has exposed mainstream economic thinking to be flawed at best and dead wrong at worst.

Historically economists have predicted interest rates by using large computer models. They spend a great deal of time discussing their complex computer-generated analyses and then predict the future interest rate simply by taking the current interest rate and assuming it will continue at that level.

They do the same thing in forecasting growth in gross domestic product (GDP). If GDP is growing at 2 percent, almost without exception all the major economists of the world making predictions about GDP growth will say that GDP will grow somewhere in the range of 1.5 to 2.5 percent. This isn't rocket science. This is the first thing you learn in business school, that predicting dramatic changes in economic conditions is difficult. So the best thing to do is just extrapolate from what you see at the moment.

But it takes only a few errant cycles to show how crazy this system is. This is crucial information for investors because almost all the advice they receive from their financial advisers and stockbrokers is based on these predictions.

To see how crazy current economic thinking is, you need only look at the ways economists suggest we get out of the current crisis. Perhaps the funniest advice, if it weren't so popular and therefore scary, is that the way to cure deficits of a government is to cut taxes. As I discussed in a previous chapter, this is the Republican line—that somehow by lowering taxes we're going to increase revenue and reduce the deficit.

We have Art Laffer of the University of Southern California to thank for this inane theory. He drew on the back of a napkin his famous Laffer curve, which showed that as you increase taxes people work less, so the economy slows and tax revenues decline. Therefore, he reasoned, if you cut taxes, people will work longer, produce more, and tax revenues will increase. This is a classic example of economic modeling. It makes for a nice paper, but it bears no relation to how things work in the real world.

It turns out that people are much more driven by relative levels of income, wealth, and taxes than they are absolute levels. Economists pretend not to understand this. Imagine a world in which the average income is $50,000 per person. From a productivity standpoint, it makes little difference in this world whether tax rates are 10 percent or 30 percent. In one case the average person brings home $45,000 a year after tax; in the other, $35,000. Laffer suggests that if people earn only $35,000 a year, they'll work less. At first blush, logic would seem to dictate that the opposite is true—they're poorer, so they would work harder to try to earn the same amount of money they were making previously. But more important, if people care more about how their incomes compare with those of their peers than about the exact dollar figure, it doesn't matter whether everyone's making $45,000 or $35,000. What they care about is outperforming their neighbor; because tax rates apply to everyone, changing tax rates does little to affect motivations of workers and thus has little impact on productivity.

History has confirmed this: When income tax rates were much higher—remember, they went as high as 90 percent in the twentieth century—people didn't work any less hard. Yes, they spent more time looking for tax loopholes, but they were still motivated to earn more than their peers.

Of course it is wealthy conservatives who constantly push this idea of lower taxes creating growth and reducing government deficits. It's not hard to see why. Wealthy conservatives benefit from lower tax rates. They earn more than their share of income. Of course corporations are constantly going to be arguing for lower corporate taxes and lower personal taxes for their executives and managers.

Meanwhile, on the left, liberal economists like Paul Krugman and Robert Reich argue that government stimulus programs and increased government spending, even if financed 100 percent with new government debt, can accelerate growth, create jobs, and reduce deficits. Liberal economists favor this theory because their constituency is full of government workers: firefighters, police officers, teachers, municipal workers, and the like.

But it makes no sense. Simple math tells you that if you spend $100 million today and borrow the $100 million from other citizens, you haven't increased the amount of economic activity at all. The $100 million you borrowed is money that those people may have spent in the real economy, and government spending tends to be some of the least efficient spending there is. Unless there is a huge multiplier effect—unless governments find enormously profitable projects to invest in—it is impossible for government stimuli financed with government debt to create long-term growth. Yes, in the very, very short run, stimulus projects may bridge a one- or one-and-a-half-year temporary decline in GDP in a recession, but we'll all pay for it later when the debt comes due. When we have to repay the debt that we borrowed to finance the stimulus, guess what? We'll be taking money out of the economy to do it, and consumption will decline. As a matter of fact, that's what we're seeing right now. Everybody's over-leveraged and has too much debt, so citizens, banks, governments, and corporations are consuming less as they try to pay down their debts.

Liberal economists also favor maintaining high government spending during a recession. They argue that if you cut government spending or lay off government employees, you'll be increasing unemployment and lowering demand. Well, of course, that's true, but think of what results. During a boom time, government adds employees and raises salaries, and then during the bust and recession, according to this thinking, it can't lay off any workers for fear of raising unemployment. So government grows during the boom and then stabilizes or continues to grow, relative to the size of the economy, during the bust. Private businesses will lay off workers, but public-sector workers will never be laid off. Not only is this inherently unfair, but over time it's a prescription for government to grow and grow and grow as a percentage of GDP, and this is never good for the private sector.

Just because government workers are the last to be laid off in a recession, when unemployment is already high because of the unemployment of private workers, does not mean that laying off those government workers is not proper. Imagine if one private industry—say, carpenters—were the last labor force to be laid off in a recession. So, before even questioning whether it's time to lay off carpenters, we observe that unemployment is higher than 9 percent. Then the carpenters' union argues that you best not lay off any carpenters because unemployment will worsen. You can see the circularity of this argument. If there's no demand for carpentry work, you have to go ahead and bite the bullet, feel the pain, and embrace the true unemployment rate. Just because government workers preserve their jobs longer than employees in the private sector during a recession does not make it the right thing for the economy to not lay off unproductive government workers.

I've already said that one of the biggest problems of this crisis is how overleveraged everyone is with debt, yet what is the prescription of many liberal economists? To increase debt further to finance these government stimulus programs. Kind of a "hair of the dog" approach. Many liberal economists have gone so far as to say deficits and debt levels don't matter in a recession. Paul Krugman continually points to the low interest rates at which the US government can borrow as a sign that the debt is not burdensome, that we could afford to borrow a great deal more. This is dangerous thinking. As I have discussed, the US debt is now 100 percent of GDP, or 600 to 700 percent of government revenues. While everyone realizes that maintaining debt levels greater than 60 percent of GDP is extremely risky and defaults often occur, Krugman points to the market interest rate of 3 percent on long-term Treasury bonds to argue that US government debt is safe. Yet we know that those interest rates can change dramatically overnight. Just look at the European countries that are in trouble. They too were borrowing at 3 to 4 percent one day and within a month or two found themselves borrowing at 19 to 20 percent. The market can be cruel when it turns on you.

Yes, the United States benefits from its size and its productive economy, and the world right now feels safe investing in US securities, but this is all relative. The choice is to invest in an overleveraged Japan, a bankrupt Europe, or a United States that appears troubled but historically has gotten through without defaulting. I believe that when people step back and realize how overleveraged the United States is, how big its deficits are, how quickly its debts are growing, how slowly it is growing, and how out of control its Medicare and Social Security spending is, they will realize that in the next five to ten years, the United States quickly could have debt-to-GDP levels of 150 to 200 percent. Certainly when that happens, people are not going to be lending the United States money at 3 percent.

Some economists out there support what the Federal Reserve has been doing, namely, printing money. Never in the history of the Federal Reserve has it given banks more than $50 billion in excess reserves. Today these excess reserves stand at $2 trillion. People mistakenly believe that banks choose to hold these monies with the Fed and that this is what creates excess reserves. Just the opposite is true. They have causality going in the wrong direction. It is the Fed that creates money out of thin air and then lends it to the banks, creating these excess reserves.

Economists must see how unfair the printing or counterfeiting of money by the Federal Reserve is. It's not just that the Fed gives these monies to member banks for free. It is that this extra currency makes all the currency you hold less valuable. You've got more currency chasing the same amount of goods, so you have to eventually have inflation. And, God forbid if you're a senior trying to get by investing in CDs earning 1 percent a year in a world where the Federal Reserve is printing 50 or 60 percent more currency each year. Finally, if you're an investor and you think you're earning a decent return of 5 or 6 percent on your $100,000 investment, in a world of high inflation, with the Federal Reserve printing money, you haven't done the analysis correctly. You might get back your 5 or 6 percent per year, but when they give you back your $100,000 at the maturity of a security, you'll find out it buys only half of what it used to. In essence, you could lose half your principal amount in purchasing power just through inflation.

The economists' silence is deafening. Most work at universities, so it is not surprising they have little to say about the dramatic increase in the cost of a college education. I went to the Anderson School of Management at UCLA, and during my second year there, I became an in-state resident and my tuition was $3,000 a year.

In-state tuition at Anderson is now $42,000 a year. UCLA's business school was a bargain when I went there, which is why it attracted so many talented students who did not have the resources to go to the Harvards and Stanfords of the world. At the time, Anderson was ranked seventh in the country. Now, having lost its tuition advantage, UCLA's business school attracts a more average group of students, and its rank has dropped out of the global top 50. Anderson's enrollment has not increased by that much, so the real question is, where have all the additional tuition dollars gone? Well, some faculty members are earning more than $200,000 to $300,000 a year, and that's just their salary. Many earn hundreds of thousands of dollars more in speaking fees, expert witness fees, partnerships with corporations and banks, and by starting their own companies while supposedly maintaining a full-time teaching load. Most economists agree that education is the key to expanding growth and development in a country. It makes no sense that these faculty members would support ever-higher costs for a college education if they were truly interested in meritocratic development.

I don't know any academics who have spoken out against the dangers of the interconnectedness of the credit default swap (CDS) market. It's so obvious to me that if all the financial institutions, insurance companies, and hedge funds of the world are tied together with cross-guarantees, none of them will default. And if any default, they all will, and this seems to violate the first premise of capitalism, that poorly performing firms have to be allowed to go bankrupt.

Finally, some smart economists are starting to recognize that the debt burden on consumers, businesses, and governments is causing consumption demand to decline rapidly and preventing a recovery, but these same economists will not speak out against bailouts that give creditors 100 cents back on each dollar of their investment. If we keep trying to bail out companies at 100 cents on the dollar, we allow no restructuring of companies' and banks' debts. There is no decline in their debt levels. The best way to get rid of a debt is to allow individuals, banks, and companies to restructure and pay creditors back pennies on the dollar. That's how you get rid of debt immediately. Yes, investors suffer, but it's a loss they've already suffered. All you're doing is recognizing that these creditors lent too much money to these entities and they're not going to be repaid. We can do it today, or we can lose one or two decades like Japan did and hide what happened for years to come.

Economists are in love with the idea of free markets and have grown up thinking that government regulation is bad.

Have they not seen what the lack of regulation, especially of banks, has done to our financial sector and our global economy? They need to reread their Economics 101 text. On page one, it clearly states, There can be no capitalism; there can be no free markets; there can be no property ownership or contracts without the rule of law and regulation. It is regulation that determines how the game is played. Without regulation, who would enforce contracts? What policing authority would there be? What court system would there be to decide disagreements? The basis of capitalism is property rights, but there can be no property rights without titling systems, mortgage and lien systems, and property records. We found this out in the worst possible way when bankers decided to foreclose on homes without having proper liens and titles.

Economists appear not to have the first clue as to why inequality is so damaging to a country. They continue to recommend tax cuts for the very wealthy, even though the wealthiest 1 percent are now bringing home 21 percent of each year's total personal income and enjoying a much larger percentage of the country's wealth than ever before. It is estimated that the top 1 percent of Americans control 35 percent of the nation's total wealth. And as noted earlier, the top 400 richest Americans have more wealth than the poorest half of all Americans, approximately 155 million people.

Economies perform best when wealth is distributed more broadly. I believe the reason is twofold. First, in order to get the most out of an electorate and a citizenry, it is important that all young people are motivated to study and educate themselves in the sincere belief that their studies will pay off with more rewarding careers.

Second, and perhaps as important, if all the wealth resides with the top 1 percent, it becomes easy for these super-wealthy people to buy Congress and even the presidency. They can do it through campaign donations, expensive lobbying campaigns, financing campaigns by phony grassroots citizen movements, or simply by spending an enormous amount of money on television advertising during the election season.

Once the wealthy control our government, they will write rules that benefit themselves and the companies, banks, and investments that they own and control. They would cut personal taxes even when government deficits are large and growing. They would be in favor of corporate tax breaks and all sorts of corporate welfare for their businesses, and they would be against any regulation that prevented them from ripping off consumers and other investors. What the wealthy most want from government is enormously destabilizing to an economy and to a democracy. To be effective, economies and social democracies have to be built on fairness, justice, and equal opportunity. Any other approach is not only inhuman and unjust, but it is bad for the country, bad for its people, bad for the economy, and, yes, bad for business.

EIGHT

WHY MARKETS DON'T BEHAVE THE WAY THEY ARE SUPPOSED TO

Markets don't behave the way they're supposed to. There are a number of crucial discrepancies between how markets work in the real world and how they work on chalkboards in academia. One of the most glaring is in the understanding of what causes booms and busts. Economists worship at the altar of equilibrium. They see economies as essentially stable, and if some unexpected jolt knocks an economy temporarily out of whack, they believe prices should adjust to retain its stability and maintain nearly full employment.

But historically this is rarely how markets work. Since the beginning of time, markets have been subject to boom-and-bust cycles. Of course behaviorists attribute this to human irrationality. They see investors and consumers as fundamentally stupid, always following Ponzi schemes and assuming that when prices go up, they will increase forever. But I, for one, certainly don't believe that and wouldn't invest my money that way. If I see an asset that has tripled in price, my natural reaction is not to assume that it will continue to increase but just the opposite—that it is now high priced relative to fundamentals and will probably decline in the future unless circumstances change dramatically.

Looking at this particular crisis, I don't believe the participants acted irrationally either. To the extent that investors lost money, I would argue it was because they were misled by criminal and corrupt behavior. If the investors had known that banks were packaging and selling mortgages that they knew were already defaulting, if investors knew that the investment bank issuing these securities was paying the rating agencies to give false hope to investors, and if investors understood that their financial advisers became rich regardless of whether their clients lost money, I think investors would have behaved differently during the boom years.

People take a great deal of comfort in knowing that they are paying a price that is determined by a market, and that it is equal to prices paid for comparable recently completed transactions. This is only reasonable because if you know other people paid good money for a similar asset, it is an indication that people in general see value there. But what this ignores is that an entire marketplace of buyers can be misled by corrupt and criminal activity. If a traditional bank you've done business with for years sells you a mortgage security, you would likely be shocked to find out that your banker was ripping you off to maximize his own short-term income.

The question still unanswered is what causes booms and busts. The truth is, we spend too much time trying to determine what causes crashes, recessions, and financial crises, when what we really need to do is analyze what causes booms. After all, as long as booms and bubbles occur, it is inevitable that the bubbles will burst and countries will enter recessions and banks will face bad loans.

So how are bubbles created? At the most basic level, they are caused by consumers spending too much for goods and buying too many of them. Almost without exception, I trace all boom periods to the commercial banks. In my lifetime alone, I have witnessed numerous booms in particular asset markets caused by overly aggressive lending by banks. Banking is a funny business. It is enormously competitive. One bank in town starts doing stupid, overly aggressive lending on overly aggressive terms. Its competitors in town must either match the first bank's stupid pricing or lose all their market share. As Citibank's chief executive officer said, "As long as the music is playing, we have to keep dancing." One banking executive almost begged the government to step in and regulate banking activity because he realized that as long as the Countrywides of the world continued to make stupid loans, others in the sector would have to match their pricing. Of course his plea was ignored.

I watched in the 1980s as banks lent way too much money to farmers based on bubble pricing of their farmland. Farmers took the cash and invested in land and farming equipment. When prices burst, the banks quickly called in many of these loans, but the farmers couldn't repay the loans quickly because the long-term assets they had invested in were difficult to sell in a tough environment. So the banks ended up foreclosing on the farmers and causing a farm crisis.

In the late 1980s, the banks did exactly the same thing in leveraged buyout lending. Originally many successful leveraged buyouts were structured such that the banks lent four to five times a company's free cash flow. But then the banks got competitive with each other and drove up the prices of leveraged buyouts, and by the late 1980s, many were closing at nine to ten times cash flow. Of course at these levels, repaying the debt is impossible. And if there is ever any future weakness in consumer demand leading to a slight recession, these overleveraged companies quickly go bankrupt, creating enormous bad loan losses for the banks.

In the early 1990s, the banks did the same thing with commercial real estate and office buildings. You couldn't accuse the property developers of being irrational. They were hardly ever using any of their own money for their development deals and for office buildings they were constructing. The banks were giving them 100 percent construction financing, and takeout financing meant to replace the bank financing with permanent capital was easily arranged. As a general rule, if you're playing with other people's money, you're not as careful as when you're spending your own, and property developers ended up wasting a great deal of money on their projects. The bubble got bigger in Houston than elsewhere, and, just before it burst, new buildings there came to be called "see-throughs" because they were never occupied and had no curtains on the windows, so from the freeway you could literally see through the buildings.

Overseas, the Japanese experienced an enormous bubble in their commercial and residential property markets in the 1990s, again financed with stupid and overly aggressive lending by their banks, which added assets so rapidly that Japan once boasted seven of the ten largest banks in the world.

A number of factors were implicated in the implosion of Long-Term Capital Management in 1996, but its almost infinite leverage was certainly the key to its quick downfall. Bankers lent the speculative hedge fund money without even asking what its total leverage was or how much money other banks had lent it.

In 1998, Thailand, Korea, and Russia collapsed because a huge amount of capital flowed into those countries that then slowed and reversed. All of Korea's Chaebols and largest businesses were dramatically overleveraged, with Daewoo and Hyundai approaching debt-leverage ratios common for leveraged buyouts in the United States.

Commercial banks cannot be blamed for the 2001 high-tech bubble and collapse, but corruption played a major role in that the investment banks were making a great deal of money by having their research analysts promote dramatically overvalued Internet stocks because they were making so much money in fees from selling those shares to the public.

The investment banks weren't stupid. They put their biggest and best institutional clients into the stocks of the initial public offerings of these high-tech companies on the first day. They undervalued these initial public offerings so their biggest institutional investors received windfall returns of 50 and 60 percent in the first week. And then, six months later, when the stock prices collapsed, all their institutional investors were magically out of the stocks, and the people left holding the bag were small, individual investors.

People now understand that in 2006 and 2007 the housing crisis was caused by way too much lending to individual homeowners. The average home in San Diego sold for 11 times a family's income. Traditionally the average ratio nationwide was 2.3 times a family's income. And, just as it proved difficult for a corporation to repay its debt from a leveraged buyout, it's very hard for a family to repay its mortgage debt if the loan was for more than five times its income. At 11 times your income, more than 60 percent of your take-home pay is going to your mortgage. This certainly is not sustainable in the long run, and it's impossible if the family faces any type of medical emergency or either of its wage earners takes a pay cut or loses a job.

What people don't realize about the crisis of 2007 is that it was not just home mortgages for which the banks lent too much money. It was not just a subprime crisis. If you looked at the banks' portfolios, they had lent too much money to everyone. Their leveraged buyout lending was being done at prices seen at the 1989 peak in leveraged buyouts, and companies were being bought with financing equal to nine or ten times the company's cash flow.

Banks were lending to hedge funds on a collateralized basis, with no appreciation that the assets used for collateral might decline in value. Banks even lent to each other in the repo market (the market for repurchase agreements), not realizing that an investment bank was financing more than half of its nightly operations with money that they had to re-finance nightly. In other words, if the investment bank wasn't creditworthy for one day, it would go bankrupt, yet its cash flows didn't necessarily have to decline for this to happen. All that had to happen was the collateral that the investment bank was posting in the repo market had to decline in value such that it was unacceptable as collateral for a repo loan, and this is exactly what happened. Once lenders don't like your collateral, they stop lending to you, and if a great majority of your firm's funding is overnight repos, you can be out of busi-ness in 24 hours.

It's incredible that European commercial banks were lever-aged 40 to 1 and that US banks were leveraged at more than 30 to 1. But even more incredible is that the investment banks, which had few assets and few depositors, were also leveraged 30 to 1. Goldman Sachs, Morgan Stanley, Lehman Brothers, and Bear Stearns were all leveraged 30 to 1. These are highly volatile businesses. They're in the business of trading securi-ties, and many had become essentially large hedge funds, in-vesting in assets and businesses for their own account. If one lost 3 percent of all its assets, the bank would lose all its equity and go bankrupt.

So what causes booms? Banks. Banks do stupid, aggres-sive lending on overly aggressive terms. Competitive banks meet that pricing and drive the entire financial sector into the ground. Of course no one complains during the bubble years. Everyone's making record bonuses and record salaries. Homeowners are out borrowing against their houses and buying new cars, vacations, and expensive dinners in fancy restaurants. Who wants to stop the party? Who wants to take away the punch bowl?

This is where government must step in. It's not in the interest of any economic participant to stop a boom. The Federal Reserve is supposed to regulate our largest banks. Without an unbiased, non-conflicted, disinterested government to monitor boom cycles, booms will continue.

The recession that inevitably follows is also caused by the banks because, as their bad loans explode, the banks pull back on their lending. There may be good projects that deserve financing from the banks that would keep the economy growing, but they can't get the money to proceed. The banks are tired of bad loans. They figure the way to get through these tough times and avoid insolvency is to hide their bad loans and continue to use exorbitant fees from their consumers and depositors over time to fund their bad loans before anyone finds out the banks are insolvent.

We're allowing this to occur even now, after the fact. We realize that the banks still have enormous bad loans on their books, yet we refuse to force them to recognize it and instead allow them to rewrite the rules such that they don't have to mark their bad assets to market. So naturally the banks delay recognition of their losses until they have income to balance those losses. What it means, of course, is the banks are not going to be aggressive lenders again for decades, guaranteeing that this recession will drag out for years and years.

The worst things that banks do in a "recovery" is to stop lending and invest their free cash flow in government securities because the Federal Reserve—again, at the banks' whim—lowers interest rates to nearly zero. The banks borrow on an almost free basis, leverage up 30 to 1, and reinvest in US Treasuries at 3 percent. Well, if your borrowing costs are near zero, and you leverage a 3 percent investment 30 to 1, you can generate 90 percent cash returns on your equity before administrative expenses. It doesn't take long to generate enormous profits that then allow you to recover your negative equity base and remain in business. It's a testament to the severity of this crisis that we are now five years out, and the banks still have not recovered all the money they lost.

Thus, booms cause busts, busts cause recessions, and recessions cause financial crises, and typically the banks are behind all of it.

There is one exception. Sometimes government itself is the culprit, which was the case in the 1970s in the United States. If the government runs deficits and prints money to fund those deficits, price inflation will occur. People ask me how it is possible to have future inflation and price appreciation if there's no consumer demand in a weak recessionary environment. I tell them that in the 1930s in the Weimar Republic in Germany, the price of a loaf of bread was increasing 500 percent per day, even though between the wars the people in Germany were so poor that few could afford to buy a loaf of bread. Similarly, in recent years in Zimbabwe, inflation approached 100,000 percent per year, yet the people had incomes of less than $50 a month and no discretionary spending to drive prices up through consumer demand.

This was the situation in the 1970s in the United States. The term *stagflation* was used to describe the period because it surprised economists that you could have dramatic price appreciation with inflation approaching 15 percent, a recession with high unemployment, and little economic growth.

The economists didn't understand that higher prices are not typically caused by greater consumer demand. Higher prices across all goods and services can be caused only by more currency chasing the same amount of goods, and the only way you have more currency is for the Federal Reserve to print money. So in the 1970s, the government printed enormous amounts of money to fund its deficits, the dollar devalued tremendously relative to a fixed asset like gold, and it caused a recession.

High inflation caused by a government printing money can cause a real economy to collapse. Monitarists just don't see this. Monitarists believe that inflation is nominal and not real, and that an economy ought to perform equally well with 2 percent inflation and 10 percent inflation because all prices are changing an equal amount.

What they don't realize is that the two biggest industries for most countries are housing and automobiles, and both are purchased by consumers on a long-term contractual basis. Home buyers sign a 30-year mortgage to buy a house, and cars are typically paid off over five to seven years. What this means is that in order to buy houses and cars, consumers have to qualify for a loan, and during periods of high inflation when interest rates approach 12 to 15 percent, it is impossible for homeowners or car buyers to qualify.

Big banks do not understand that during high inflationary periods, the value of houses and home buyers' wages will also increase, making their loans safe, and so the big banks constrict the amount of money they lend, causing those two major industries, home building and automobile sales, to collapse. Once home building, home renovation, furniture sales, and new car sales collapse, the entire economy follows. You cannot have a weak housing sector and a weak automobile sector and a strong economy, given how many Americans these industries employ. So in this unique case, the government, rather than the banks, caused the boom, bust, and recession.

There are many other reasons that markets in the real world don't behave like their theoretical constructs in the classroom, and lately these exceptions have become more the rule. One of the biggest is market manipulation. Market manipulation is a criminal and corrupt form of cheating that is not only illegal but is basically presumed not to occur in a developed market.

But in our country, hedge funds are not transparent in any way. They don't have to report any of their activity, and they are never investigated. Not that all hedge funds cheat, but unscrupulous fund managers certainly do—they know there is no chance they will ever be investigated.

Some hedge funds specialize in the trading of one or two securities, and what they do, even though they are not large firms, is dominate the trading activity in a particular stock or bond. Because they are "the market," they basically control the market. Thus, you no longer have a free market. The assumption that all the buyers and sellers are acting independently and ethically completely falls apart. We've seen many examples of this market manipulation over time. Individual companies' CEOs have complained that hedge funds are crushing their stocks, trading them up and down each day just to create volatility and opportunities for the hedge fund to get in and out at a profit.

Even worse, individual commodities like coffee, silver, or even oil appear to be subject to enormous speculation and market manipulation. Oil prices boomed during the early days of this crisis and then collapsed. I could see no rational reason for oil prices' tripling to more than $150 a barrel when the economy was weakening, and the demand for oil was sure to decline in a global recession. I believe that the price of oil might have been manipulated, probably not by one hedge fund but in a collusive effort by some of the largest hedge funds and perhaps working closely with the investment and commercial banks.

Perhaps the most egregious form of cheating in a free market is insider trading. Academics dismiss it as just an efficient way of getting new information to a market. They like the idea that the market price reflects not only public information but insider information as well, and they call this strong-form efficiency.

What the academics fail to recognize is that once a market is tainted with insider trading, investors just don't trust it anymore. Who would want to play a game in which the other participants are trading on information unavailable to you? It is as if you were playing online poker and you found out that the other eight people at the table were all in a room together and sharing their hands with each other. Or, worse, as reportedly occurred with one online poker company, you find out that the company running the site is looking at everybody's hand and also playing against you at the table.

Now, economists may applaud insider trading as increasing information efficiency, but what they fail to see is that, if people and small investors believe that a market is rigged and others have access to information that they do not and can trade on it, then small investors will pull back from the market and you'll have no market at all. Why would you buy IBM stock in the market if the seller already knows what IBM's earnings announcement is going to say tomorrow? And if the seller knows IBM's earnings are going to be incredibly bad, he will be selling into your bid and you'll end up owning IBM the day before it disappoints investors with its earnings announcement.

I believe the reason that markets are performing so badly today and are such a poor indicator of true asset values is that the markets are corrupt. There are a thousand different ways to cheat, but the simplest way is nontransparency. If you're buying bank stocks and the banks are lying about their financial condition and the amount of their bad loans, how can you possibly properly evaluate that bank? Similarly, if the banks have enormous derivatives exposure that is not disclosed properly in their financial reporting, how can you properly evaluate the prospects for those banks?

Just because a market is volatile does not mean that it's corrupt. In 2011 alone, there were many days, back to back, when the Dow Jones Industrial Average jumped and then plummeted 500 points. Because we see little new information in the marketplace, we presume that somebody is either manipulating stock prices or that high-frequency trading or other hedge fund activity is causing dislocations in the market. But this doesn't necessarily have to be true.

It turns out that there really are two states of a free economy. A free economy can be in a normal equilibrium stage or it can collapse, thanks to banks and governments, into a recession and financial crisis. If, indeed, a country goes into a recession, corporate earnings can decline as much as 30 to 40 percent, and companies' growth prospects can evaporate. Properly valuing a publicly traded company as a country enters a recession, given its lower earnings and growth prospects, could mean that its stock should trade at 40 to 50 percent less than in more normal times.

And so when we see the stock market jump up and down by 3, 4, and 5 percent a day, it's not necessarily because of manipulation. It could be the market's attempt to decide whether we're entering a recession. In any one day, if the probability of a recession has increased by 5 percent because Europe can't straighten out its debt problems or because the banks continue not to recognize their loan losses, then the values of stocks should change by a 5 percent probability that a recession will occur and their prices in that recession will decline by 50 percent. Five percent probability times 50 percent possible price declines means you might see daily declines of 2.5 to 3 percent, and that's exactly what we saw in 2011.

I understand that thus far I've spent a great deal of space in this book describing general economic conditions and theories about stock market efficiencies and economist theories of booms and busts and the outlooks for the United States and the rest of the developed world, but this is essential to investors. You have to understand the environment in which you are investing. Once you realize that there are going to be continued troubled times ahead, and that this market itself is not fair to individual investors, you must look elsewhere to invest your money. The idea that you will passively just ride out any recession is wrongheaded.

Yes, buy-and-hold strategies have worked historically in the United States because in the past the United States has always recovered, but it certainly hasn't worked in countries that didn't recover. There are lots of examples where countries became more and more corrupt, their financial system collapsed, and their stock markets went bad and never recovered—think Russia in 1998, Argentina in 2001, and Iceland in 2008. I'm not suggesting that the United States won't some day recover, but it's going to take an enormous reform effort, which I don't see happening in the near future. We are going to have to pull ourselves out of this global recession, which is going to be extremely difficult given how wedded our elected officials are to big campaign contributions from banks and big corporations.

Let me now turn to traditional investments that most investors hold. I will show you that they are poorly structured to deal with the corrupt environment around the world and the global recession, which is nowhere near an end. Once you understand that traditional investments like stocks and bonds and government securities such as US Treasuries and even money market funds won't cut it as successful investments in the future, you will begin to understand what the real threats are to your investment portfolio and what you need to do to protect yourself.

NINE

WHY STOCKS, BONDS, AND MONEY MARKETS WON'T CUT IT

I t's time to disabuse you of the notion that your money is safe in stocks, corporate or municipal bonds, or even money market funds. That way it will be easier to convince you to move your money into nontraditional, nonfinancial assets. In the next chapter, I will try to convince you that your money is not even safe in US Treasury securities or the government securities of other countries. But never fear—there are alternatives.

I'll start with stocks. I've already covered some of the problems here. Stocks are subject to insider trading and market manipulation. If you invest in stocks yet cannot analyze the company properly because the companies either don't report correctly or cheat or withhold information about their bad loans and bad assets, you're a dupe. And, as we all know, if you sit down at a poker table and you can't figure out who the dupe is, it's probably you.

Second, the biggest problem with stocks is that they are by definition plays on the underlying economy. When the economy does well, corporate profits grow, margins increase, and cash flows increase and stock prices do better as a result. But in a weak recessionary environment with no recovery in the near future, it is hard to imagine how corporate profits will grow. Corporations hope to grow by hiring workers overseas and lowering their expense costs and by selling products overseas so as not to be tied to the US economy.

Unfortunately, we're running out of countries that are not in recession with their own consumer demand evaporating. China was the last to go, but in the third quarter of 2011, even China announced its annual growth rate in GDP had declined from 11 percent to 7 percent, and even that was probably overstated. The real growth rate was probably 3 percent because it appears that China understated its inflation rate by four percentage points (Keith Bradsher, "Rising Chinese Inflation to Show Up in U.S. Imports," *New York Times,* January 11, 2011).

If a country understates its inflation rate and then reports its inflation-adjusted growth, by definition it's overstating its real growth rates. So even overseas, there isn't a strong market for US corporations to sell into. The world's biggest markets are the United States and Europe, and they're both on the operating table not looking good. So stocks are subject to busts, recessions, and crises in a very real way because they're tied directly to corporate earnings, which are tied to the real economy. Right now, the last thing you want to do is to be an equity partner in that type of economy. I would avoid all stocks.

Never before have stocks been so dramatically different an investment than bonds. Historically they were just different investment layers of the same company. Now, Geithner, Paulson, and the European Union have decided that stock prices of troubled companies can plummet into the single digits, but bonds will always be paid off at par.

The powers that be made an exception in the case of Greece, where they're allowing some private investors to take a 50 percent haircut, but Greece is small potatoes compared with the countries they're actually worried about, such as Italy and Spain. I can assure you they will not allow a large country to default because it would cause German and French banks to default, and that would take the German and French governments down with them.

Even the Greek default is kind of a joke because they're calling it voluntary on behalf of the creditors, and so they're claiming that there is no default for credit default swap (CDS) purposes. So all those people who bought insurance against a Greek default are going to watch creditors get paid back 50 cents on the dollar, and they won't receive a dime from the insurance they bought in the CDS market. It's another classic case of why insurance is a terrible investment. You pay your premiums during good times, and in bad times the insurance company finds some crazy reason not to honor its policy.

Greater shareholder representation on boards would also go a long way toward correcting improper and ineffective corporate and bank management. Much of the reason to buy both stocks and bonds in the past was the theory of diversification, peddled almost universally by financial advisers. In a later chapter, I'll discuss a major problem with this theory, which says the more diversified you are, the less risk you have, the more risk-adjusted return you earn, and the better off you are.

The truth is, economists completely miss a second-tier effect of diversification, which I believe is more damaging to the global economy than any minor benefits that accrue from a diversified portfolio. By diversifying and holding hundreds, if not thousands, of different assets all around the world, in stocks and bonds and real estate and commodities, you end up with a portfolio so large and diverse that you couldn't possibly properly evaluate each asset, and you would never have the time to supervise the management of each of the companies. Thorough diversification by institutional investors, and now by individual investors through mutual funds and index funds, ensures that crummy, ineffective, and corrupt managements are free to loot a company of its assets without any involvement by the shareholders.

Of course no other market is more heavily researched by analysts and traders than the stock market. This used to be good news—the companies were well researched, and their stock prices reflected all available information, so there were few surprises and few volatile days in individual stock prices. Nowadays it means just the opposite—more Wall Street traders are out there looking for ways to rip off small investors, and more stock analysts are constantly hectoring CEOs and CFOs for inside information that they can use against you, the small investor.

We are just now discovering the dangers of high-frequency traders. We don't know how much of the current volatility in the stock market they cause. But think about it. Efficiency in a market means that one entity is not supposed to be able to constantly win. The reason that high-frequency traders show unusual profits every quarter, which violates any sense of efficiency in a market, is because they're trading faster than anybody else. They don't necessarily have to trade on nonpublic information; they're just trading faster than anyone else possibly could on public information.

Literally within seconds of a public announcement by a publicly traded company, these high-frequency traders have already adjusted their portfolios and either bought or sold more of that particular stock. Legally they're trading on public information, but at that point it's public only to them and their superfast computers. It won't be available *to you* on your computer screen for minutes or even hours when you can call your broker and react to it. They live in milliseconds, and you live in minutes.

I'm trying to think of another game as unfair as this. All I can think of is two baseball teams, one that gets to use tennis rackets to bat with while the other has to use broomsticks. You can keep score if you want, but I think I already know which team is going to win that game.

Investors should realize that stocks also face a problem shared by bonds and money market funds—all three investments here in the United States are dollar denominated. You may think you're properly diversified and protected until you realize that, because of the corrupt printing of money by the Federal Reserve, the dollar has devalued dramatically over time.

The dollar can decline relative to other currencies, but this isn't even necessary for the dollar to lose value. If other countries of the world are also rapidly expanding their currency, there will be no dramatic change in the exchange rate between currencies, but it doesn't mean the dollar is not

losing purchasing power. The way to think about it, as I'll discuss in Chapter 13, is to compare the value of the dollar with a
more fixed wealth asset that retains its value better over time.
(I think gold is the best asset for this purpose, and later I will
describe why I think gold is much more stable than the currencies of individual countries.)

So that pretty much does it for stocks. If you still want to
go invest in an index or money market fund and think you'll
be protected because you're diversified, I have news for you.
You're not diversified across currencies. You're not protected
against inflation.

Academics have studied how stocks react to unanticipated inflation, and even though stocks represent ownership
in real companies, their stocks do poorly when inflation reignites. This is because, as I discussed earlier, during periods
of high inflation, new home construction and car purchases
decline dramatically because they are contract purchases,
and the high interest rate environment of an inflationary period prevents people from qualifying for home loans and car
loans. And once these two sectors collapse, the entire economy follows.

You should gain no comfort from being diversified because in tough times, correlations all go to one. In good times,
different stocks move in different directions, and by diversifying you decrease the overall risk of your portfolio, whereas in
tough times or illiquid times, financial crises assets tend to

move together. And so diversification has little benefit. Even strong stocks of large, successful, and highly profitable companies do poorly in crises because they're the only stocks that have any liquidity and any buyers. A hedge fund or a leveraged bank that is in trouble and needs to raise cash quickly doesn't sell its holdings in illiquid smaller company stocks; it sells it's big company holdings because it can, and their value decreases. There is no market for its less liquid, smaller holdings.

Let me move on to bonds. Any long-term fixed-rate bond investment is subject to inflation risk, and the risk is that you will lose a large percentage of your purchasing power when your principal is returned. It's even worse than the stock market because you have all the downside risk of inflation but none of the upside potential of owning a stock if things turn around and the economy improves. To me fixed-rate long-term bonds are the stupidest investment around because you have this one-sided equation where you suffer all the losses a stock might have if inflation reignites but enjoy none of the upside benefits if the economy improves.

This is why I'm always surprised, as economies head into crises and recessions, that financial advisers tell investors to move their assets from stocks into bonds. I understand what *investors* are thinking; they're thinking that the stocks are going to do poorly in an environment of lower corporate earnings, and the bonds will do fine because they've promised you a fixed return. But that fixed return is in nominal dollars only. The bond issuer has not guaranteed to protect your purchasing power. Say you have just locked in to a bond paying 5 percent per year. If inflation reignites and interest rates go to 12 percent and you're earning only 5 percent, that bond is going to collapse in value. And if you hold it until maturity, as I have said, you're going to lose a significant amount of your purchasing power. You'll get your $1,000 back that you invested in the bond, but it won't buy more than $500 or $600 worth of goods and services because of the higher prices postinflation.

I think that bonds, even more than stocks, have a huge middleman problem, which adds not only costs to the entire structure of the purchase but an entire layer of potential corruption because middlemen in the bond market definitely do not have the same incentives as you to maximize your upside and minimize your downside.

Corporate bonds and tax-free municipals have real default risk associated with them. Again, people are attracted to tax-free municipals not just because the interest is tax free but because historically few cities, housing authorities, and other municipal issuers have defaulted on their debts. But don't be fooled by this historical argument. Municipalities are in serious trouble in this recession because their property tax revenues are evaporating as housing prices decline. Sales tax revenues are declining because consumption is off dramatically, and local income taxes are declining because people are unemployed and their wages are dropping.

And all of this is occurring in an environment in which more municipal workers are retiring and claiming big pension and health-care benefits. It is pennywise and pound foolish to invest in tax-free municipals and garner an extra 1 percent by avoiding paying taxes that would otherwise go to government to help offset the risk of default.

As with stocks, bonds in the United States are dollar denominated, so you face all the risks of holding the dollar currency if it devalues in the future. Again, that devaluation is not just relative to other currencies but to purchasing power and to real assets like gold. It does you no good to earn a profit in dollars if all other assets you might purchase have grown in price so much that their price increase dwarfs the percentage profit you recognized on your bond.

Don't think you can escape these fates by moving to other countries, even emerging economies. Europe is in worse shape than the United States from both an economic and a debt perspective. And Japan is more highly leveraged than both the United States and Europe.

A lot of financial analysts are hoping the emerging countries of China and India can pull the world out of global recession. Nothing could be further from the truth. China and India act as manufacturing and service centers for the developed worlds of the United States and Europe. If our demand evaporates, their manufacturing will necessarily slow. While it is true that we've shipped almost all our manufacturing overseas to China and India, most of the exports from China and India are intracompany. They go from IBM China to IBM in the United States. In effect all we've done is outsource our manufacturing ability, but the demand is still in the United States and Europe. China does not have enough domestic demand. You sometimes hear that China has average incomes of $6,000 or $7,000 per capita, but this number is calculated on a purchasing power parity basis that adjusts for the lower cost of living in China. The correct number to look for this analysis is the market currency exchange rate of their GDP per person or income per person, and here the average Chinese is earning approximately $2,500 a year.

China and India, while enormous countries both geographically and in population, still do not have large enough economies to pull the world out of recession. If you want to be a very long-term investor, it might make some sense to put money in the stock markets of China and India, but doing so carries serious risks in the short run. India has an enormous problem in expanding its economic development beyond its privileged, educated class to the hundreds of millions of peasants in the rural areas, and China, regardless of how it positions itself as a market economy, is still a communist dictatorship with no labor unions, no press freedoms, and little Internet freedom. A country of 1.4 billion people is controlled by 20 members of the Communist Party at the top. As long as they keep making smart decisions, the country will grow. But when they make a bad decision, they have no feedback from the people working through democratic processes to tell them that they erred.

The history of countries that are managed from the top down is they do fine for a while and then they make a terrible management mistake and explode. The classic example I like to use is Japan before World War II. Japan was growing rapidly as an industrial power and had a centrally planned economy: The government told the banks, which told the corporations, exactly where to invest and where to borrow. Then the military got involved with the management of Japan, and some small number of generals came up with the brilliant idea to bomb Pearl Harbor. Whatever good growth was created by this tight, tough, central management during the 1930s was completely lost with this one stupid decision. That is the nature of dictatorships. Like a football team with an obstinate coach, the organization *seems* to be run efficiently until the coach makes a really stupid call, and then you wish that the players or the fans had a vote in the decision.

My discussion of traditional investments would not be complete without mentioning money market funds. Each money market fund is different, but they all suffer the same problem that I described earlier with banks—that is, money market funds are in competition with each other. And the advisers and managers of money market funds are not playing with their own money; they're playing with your money. They're getting paid on the upside. They're getting paid salaries and bonuses, but if things explode and you lose 20 or 30 percent of your money in their fund, they won't lose. Only you will.

So their incentives are different from yours, and I would argue that their incentives are terribly placed. What often happens is that one money market fund announces that instead of paying 1 percent—which, let's assume, is the industry average—it's going to start paying 1.1 percent. And it accomplishes this by not holding your money in cash accounts at banks but moving into alternative investments like European bank debt and subordinated debt and guaranteed investment contracts and other slightly riskier products. So their competitors match their aggressive strategy and find their own more risky assets in which to invest.

Before the crisis, this escalated so far that some money market funds were taking your cash and securities and lending them out overnight to investment banks and then taking the cash they received on a nightly basis and investing it in mortgage securities. These money market funds ended up losing much of the money they invested, and it wasn't even theirs to begin with.

The only thing that prevented the money market industry from going bankrupt was the US government's coming in and guaranteeing all money market funds. That's not safe investing, and investors should be very careful when they think their money market funds are held in cash. You, as investors, should absolutely ask your financial advisers what types of investments are allowed in their money market funds. I think you will be surprised.

It's natural, when people get nervous in tough times, to sell their stocks and maybe even their long-term bonds and move into what they consider to be cash. But if they consider money market funds cash, they need to do much more investigation as to what securities are in those funds. Some money market funds hold long-term bonds. So what's the point of selling your long-term bonds and moving into a money market if the money market itself holds long-term bonds? Anyway, you need to investigate this because it's the next great disaster. And when it happens, we'll have no excuse for being fooled because it already blew up once in 2008.

If I've convinced you that the traditional investments of stocks, corporate bonds, tax-free municipals, and even money market funds aren't as safe as they appear to be, I've done my job. It has been my objective in this chapter to put the fear of God in you. No one can predict the future with certainty, but what I'm telling you is this: If the market has troubles, if the economy continues to suffer, and if the global financial system stays under pressure because these European and American banks have not fully disclosed their losses in mortgages and now have huge losses in countries that are going bankrupt, then it's not a question of predicting *whether* these events will occur, it's making sure you understand what your investment portfolio will do under these conditions. If you realize your portfolio is exposed to a weak economic recovery and the corruption of the banking and governmental systems, you can do something about it.

TEN

ONLY AN IDIOT WOULD LEND TO A SOVEREIGN GOVERNMENT

I hope the title of this chapter got your attention. You'll notice that I didn't limit this discussion to Greece or Portugal or Italy or Spain. I'm also talking about Germany and France and the United Kingdom and Japan and especially the United States.

Historically people have felt quite comfortable lending to sovereign countries. There are a number of reasons for this. One, the countries were big. They were bigger than any corporation that people might lend to, or any bank, and this bigness gave people comfort. Second, as Walter Wriston, the CEO of Citibank in the 1970s, famously said, "Companies go bankrupt. Countries don't." Thus, he led American banks into massive lending to Latin American countries, an exercise that ended in the Latin American debt crisis in the 1980s. People often get into investing trouble when they assume that just because something hasn't happened in the past, it can't happen in the future. Housing prices didn't decline for decades, so they couldn't possibly decline in the future; AAA-rated securities never went bankrupt; and few countries in the history of the world have defaulted on their debts.

But another reason that investors felt comfortable lending to countries was that historically the countries were big relative to their debts. Years ago countries like the United States had much less debt outstanding. Of course World War II drove the debt up temporarily, but in the postwar period, it has been unusual for the US debt to exceed 25 percent of GDP. Finally, people felt more comfortable lending to countries rather than companies because countries had taxing authority. It was presumed that if they ever ran out of money, they would just raise taxes and raise more revenue. Famous last words.

As you know, the world has changed dramatically. In the developed world, countries are still quite large but not relative to their debt. We have seen that the United States has debt equal to 100 percent of its GDP. Germany and France are north of 80 percent debt to GDP, and Japan has more than 230 percent debt to GDP. The major advantage of lending to a country is now gone. You can no longer say that country debts are small relative to the size of the country. And it's hard to come up with another good reason to lend to a large leveraged country.

These countries also face enormous operating deficits and are having a difficult time raising revenues in a global recession. These deficits compund year after year to increase each country's debt, so it is hard to imagine countries' debt-to-GDP ratios doing anything but increasing in the future. This is especially true when you realize the baby boom is retiring. These countries will lose the production and tax base of the baby-boom workers, and when they retire, these governments will face the costs of funding the retirement and health-care benefits of not only their public employees but many of their private citizens.

Some lenders to sovereign nations gain comfort from the knowledge that countries can always print more currency to fund their debts. If you're lending on a long-term fixed-rate basis and you look to the government's printing money as an escape mechanism, you might be in trouble. The reason is that, as I noted earlier, the printing of money causes inflation. Inflation causes interest rates to increase. And when interest rates increase, your fixed-return security will decline in value. If you had to sell it quickly, you would lose money in the marketplace, and if you held it to maturity to avoid a short-term loss, you might receive your principal back, but it would have dramatically lost much of its purchasing power because of inflation.

Another obvious deterrent to buying a nation's securities, one that seems to occur to few people, is that you cannot take a country to bankruptcy court. These countries make their own rules. Certainly bankruptcy rules written to apply to companies make little sense when applied to countries. So, if you lend to a country and it fails to repay you, you may have little legal recourse.

If a country gets in trouble, unlike a company, it can't just sell off assets or spin off divisions. It doesn't have any divisions. It can get pretty messy when a country tries to sell the few assets that are publicly owned. Can you imagine the United States selling Yellowstone Park to France, for example? In an attempt to deleverage, the Greeks now are talking about selling assets, but I think they would have a revolt on their hands if they sold any of the Greek islands or rented out the Acropolis.

Also, unlike companies in financial difficulty, countries can't merge with a stronger country. It is not unusual for companies, if they get in over their heads in debt, to find a merger partner bigger and stronger than themselves to fold into. The debt gets assumed by the larger company and typically gets paid off 100 cents on the dollar, which is a windfall for debt holders. Many companies that get in trouble have debt trading in the marketplace at 65 cents or 70 cents on the dollar and then overnight announce a merger with a much larger, healthier company, and their debt shoots back up to 100 cents on the dollar. I guess the exception to this rule, when it comes to countries, is East Germany's merger with West Germany in 1990, but that was a reunification, and it's hard to imagine France buying Germany, the United States buying Greece, or China taking over California.

This brings us to another difference between companies in trouble and countries in trouble. Countries can't go public. Countries can't issue equity to pay down debt and reduce their leverage. There is no such concept as equity in a country. So debt is permanent and can be suffocating.

Countries also have much more difficulty than companies in downsizing. Certainly a country couldn't reduce its population, at least not morally. And when a country tries to reduce its workforce, its employees often take to the streets, protesting and striking. Also, when a significant percentage of government workers is laid off, it can cause a deepening spiral in which those layoffs weaken consumer demand, and what was a troubled financial situation turns into a deep recession with little to no growth, making debt repayment even more difficult.

Many companies have weak managements, and these are the ones most likely to get into trouble with too much debt. But even the weakest corporate management is still way more efficient than most sovereign governments. Because the large countries of the world are mostly democracies, decision making is not instantaneous or hierarchical. Democracies typically muddle through. They are poorly structured for the quick day-to-day decision making required of an entity that is overleveraged and facing burdensome monthly interest costs.

I don't want to say that members of Congress are any stupider than company CEOs, but certainly their strengths are not in financial management; after all, managing the finances of a country is just one job that members of Congress and presidents have. They have many other constituencies to worry about besides their country's debt holders—citizens, banks, corporations, the elderly, the sick, and the poor.

Governments, by definition, are not in business for profit. They don't have a bottom line. This is precisely why they are *more* likely, rather than less likely, than a company to get in trouble with their debts. Governments don't even focus on their financial position monthly, much less quarterly, and their reporting system would embarrass any company accountant. They don't separate out capital spending from operating expenditures, and their GDP measurements include all economic activity, regardless of whether it's a cost to the government, revenue, a capital expense, or a transfer payment.

Given that governments today are not so big relative to their debts, investors have few reasons to buy their securities.

But because, historically, people considered countries as good bets and not subject to default, people continue to not only invest in country debt but run to it during troubled times, when they sell out of their stock portfolios and unload their corporate debt investments. They run to put their money in US Treasury securities and the securities of other supposedly stable countries.

But like every other "unforeseen event" I've discussed here, just because major countries of the world, including the United States and Japan, have never defaulted, it doesn't mean they can't do it in the future. And as we'll see when we talk about inflation and real assets, these big countries probably won't default in total. Rather, they will print so much money and cause such a devaluation of their currency and such a diminution of value of their citizens' wealth that it will in effect be a partial default.

So let me now turn the discussion to the US Treasury market and why US Treasuries, while considered a risk-free investment, are really nothing of the sort. Even US Treasury securities have real risk attached to them. First of all, Treasuries carry some level of default risk because the country could try to claim bankruptcy or insolvency. Historically this has been a low-probability event, so Treasury investors might have received less than ten basis points, or a tenth of 1 percent per year, to take on this default risk. I would argue that this is an extremely small premium to receive as an investor in US Treasury securities today, considering what I think is a real risk of default. I don't think there's a 30 percent chance the United States will default on its debts, but even if it's a one-in-a-hundred chance over the next five years, that tells you the default-risk premium ought to be 20 basis points not ten basis points. If you think there's a 5 percent chance the United States will default, then you might require as much as 1 percent a year in a default-risk premium before you become interested in purchasing these securities.

A much greater price threat to a fixed-income, long-term Treasury investment, such as buying ten-year, fixed-rate Treasury bonds, is inflation. People really underestimate inflation when doing any type of investment analysis. As I said, people will argue for hours with an investment adviser about whether they're receiving 2.5 percent or 2.6 percent on their bond portfolio but ignore the real possibility that inflation could reignite and they could lose 50 percent of their principal's purchasing power. On a $100 investment in a Treasury bond, the difference is between receiving $2.50 a year versus $2.60 a year; the argument ignores the real risk that inflation will jump to 10 percent a year and your principal will have a purchasing power of $50, not $100. So if you want to buy Treasury securities, you need to be sure that the interest that will be paid each year will cover the expected amount of inflation. If all goods are going to increase in price by 10 percent a year, your Treasury securities better yield at least 10 percent a year.

A lot of people don't realize there's another component, also involving inflation, to getting a fair yield on a Treasury security investment. Even if inflation is currently zero, you should receive a premium on your investment in Treasury securities just for taking on the risk that inflation will reignite in the future. Even if everybody's best guesses of what inflation might be in the future is zero, there's going to be a distribution around that expected value, meaning that under different states of the world, inflation might be high and it might be low. Because there is volatility, there is risk. If you could be certain of what your returns are going to be and that your purchasing power is going to be preserved, there would be no risk. But if you're uncertain about what inflation will be in the future, you are owed an inflation-risk premium as well as compensation for the expected value of the future inflation.

Finally, when you invest in Treasury securities, you're foregoing the opportunity to invest in the economy. So if the economy is growing and other investors are achieving positive, real returns by investing in the stock market and real assets, there's an opportunity cost to investing in Treasuries, the missed opportunity to garner this real return. Therefore, in a rapidly growing, highly productive economy, you should garner a real return for investing in Treasuries, even though the security itself is not necessarily producing any real profits.

So you can see that 2 or 3 percent over the next 10 to 20 to 30 years is not the proper Treasury yield. Rather, you ought to receive at least 2 percent as a real return for foregoing other opportunities, and I would argue that you should receive another 0.5 percent return for taking on the risk that the US government will claim bankruptcy. Then you might claim another 1 to 1.5 percent (because of the volatility of unknown inflation), bringing your total required return up to 4 percent. And I would argue that instead of looking at historical or current inflation, you ought to be compensated for your best estimate of what inflation is going to be over the next 20 years—and, by my calculations, that is north of 5 percent a year and could approach 10 percent a year. So that tells me that the right long Treasury yield today ought to be something like 8 to 12 percent per year. That people are lending money to the US government at 3 percent for 30 years tells me that Treasuries are hugely overvalued, and it will be the next great bubble to burst.

When you borrow monies, it's the same thing as shorting Treasuries. When you long a security you own it outright, and when you short a security, in this case Treasuries, then you receive the monies now but owe the interest rate on it just like a borrower. So if the Treasury market is overvalued right now and in a bubble, you want to short it. This means you want to be a borrower, and you want to be a fixed-rate borrower for a long period, like 30 years. And this opportunity, which I will discuss in Chapter 12, is only available to individuals if they are homeowners.

ELEVEN

WHY DIVERSIFICATION WON'T HELP

Investors have been sold two big lies over the years: a buy-and-hold strategy is always best, and diversification leads to higher risk-adjusted returns.

I'm not a big enough conspiracy nut to think this was intentional, but it is quite damaging. Such advice encourages the majority of investors to be completely passive in their investment style. Buy and hold suggests that once you purchase a security, you hold it for life. Nothing could be more passive. And diversification gives false confidence to investors that they need do nothing else to their portfolio than sit back and enjoy pleasant returns.

Of course, this so-called wisdom didn't come out of nowhere. There is some logic to both strategies. Buy and hold became a popular strategy because stockbrokers were churning accounts and turning over portfolios every three months in order to generate more trading commissions. If you look at investors who succeed over a long period of time, the two things they do very well are manage brokerage commissions to keep them at a minimum and pay as little tax as possible, as late as possible. To a great degree, buy-and-hold strategies accomplish these two ends.

Similarly, some sophisticated mathematics demonstrate that a well-diversified portfolio achieves the greatest risk-adjusted return where risk is measured as the overall variability of your entire portfolio, not the variability of any one stock.

But I've always suspected the math that encourages ever-greater diversification has a fatal flaw. It is true that individual stocks are much more volatile than the overall market because individual factors such as oil prices affect individual stocks, such as those of oil companies, more than they affect the overall stock market. By holding all stocks, you minimize the impact of oil price shocks because you hold not just oil producers but many corporations that use oil as a source of energy in their manufacturing process. In effect you've hedged variations in the price of oil out of your portfolio by including both suppliers and users.

Diversification has the same effect on other variables. Similarly, by diversifying your portfolio across all stocks, you end up hedging out other variables that may influence the returns you generate in your portfolio. When you think about it, most banks are lenders. They benefit from a higher interest-rate environment, whereas other stocks in your portfolio may be net borrowers and so benefit from lower interest rates. Again, by holding both banks and leveraged corporations, you net out the effect of interest-rate movements in your portfolio.

The one variable almost impossible to hedge is labor, that is, labor costs and labor productivity. Almost all businesses see increased labor costs as an expense to their operation and damaging to their profitability. The perfect hedge to this, of course, is to hedge your exposure to rising labor costs by purchasing members of that workforce itself, a strategy that does better as wages rise. But that's difficult to do because slavery is illegal in all advanced countries.

Because almost all inputs to the production process are revenues to suppliers, almost all of these commodity costs and economic inputs can be hedged out of a diversified portfolio. You are left with a diversified portfolio with only one big risk, labor productivity and wage rates.

But so what? Who wants that type of portfolio? Just as someone who buys oil company stocks and doesn't diversify is making a bet that oil prices will increase in the future, some-one who holds this well-diversified portfolio is making a bet that wage rates will suffer in the future and labor productiv-ity will increase but go unrewarded. I don't see any difference in the two bets. The reason that diversified portfolios have historically outperformed single stocks in the United States is that labor productivity has improved dramatically over the last 70 years, and wage rates have stagnated over the last 30 years. If wage rates in the United States had kept up with infla-tion over the last 30 years, corporate profits would have stag-nated, and the Dow Jones Industrials wouldn't have increased in real value at all. So the reason that a diversified portfolio has done well is that US labor productivity has increased and gone unrewarded by higher wages.

The one hard-and-fast rule of investing is that if you don't take any risk, you generate no return. If you really could cre-ate a perfectly diversified portfolio, it should generate zero re-turn, about as worthwhile to you as sticking your money in a mattress. There would be no reason to invest. It's not as if you have a view on a particular company or a particular economic climate or forecast, or you think that a particular commodity price will increase or decrease in the future. If you don't have any particular view on any company's potential profitability, it doesn't make sense to me to be holding stocks, even on a di-versified basis. Why subject yourself to the up and down vari-ability of labor productivity needlessly?

I'm not throwing out the concept of diversification entirely. I readily admit that by holding ten or 12 stocks you are much better protected against individual stock shocks than by holding one or two. But there is no reason to hold hundreds or thousands of stocks, and certainly there is no reason to hold investments across all countries and asset classes.

Even when I was in business school, I was uncomfortable with the theoretical concept that diversification maximizes risk-adjusted returns. Certainly it limits your upside because when you have a good idea and invest only 10 percent of your money in it because you want to stay diversified, and it doubles in value, your portfolio increases only 10 percent. Whereas if you take all your money and invest it in that good idea and it doubles, you double the value of your portfolio. So diversification limits downsides, but it also limits upsides.

Diversification theory has an additional weakness, which is especially glaring today. It assumes you don't have to do any financial analysis because all markets are perfectly efficient, and therefore there is no risk of your overpaying for an individual stock. Someone else has already done the analysis and incorporated all publicly available information into the stock price and made sure the stock price is properly valued relative to the company's earnings. It is a defeatist, passive attitude that you never have an idea that can make money in the investment market. You are presumed to be ignorant, to not be able to read newspapers or financial reports, and to not have a view of whether it's appropriate to buy or sell an individual stock.

The danger of this approach is that it fosters a belief that market prices are always right. This is what got homeowners into trouble during the housing crash. Homeowners weren't completely stupid. They didn't immediately spend all the money the banks gave them. They looked around their neighborhood and saw that other homes similar to theirs were being bought and sold at prices relative to the square footage and relative to potential rental income from the property at levels close to what they were paying for their home. Who would have thought that an entire market, nationally and internationally, could be overpriced? But this is the net effect of banks' lending too much money on loose terms, and it drives a stake through the heart of the theory that market prices are always right.

Finally, this crisis has exposed another fallacy of diversification. Finance experts used to believe that the best way to measure volatility of individual assets was to check the history of how they reacted to different price shocks over an extended period. Now, thanks to Long-Term Capital Management's experience in 1996, and to what happened to almost all stock, bond, and credit markets in this financial crisis in 2008, economists understand that individual assets don't necessarily move counter to each other during tough times. In financial crises and severe recessions, liquidity dries up. Banks pull back on all lending, and firms have real difficulty financing their port-folios, especially hedge funds, commercial banks, and invest-ment banks that borrow very short term in the overnight repo market to buy long-term assets such as stocks and bonds. What in fact happens is that all stocks, bonds, and commodities be-gin to trade down together. There is no countervailing influ-ence between different holdings that minimizes risk.

Instead, correlations go to one. This means the variability lines up across different assets, and they all go down together. Well, if all your assets will go down during a crisis (and a crisis is the most important time period you want to evaluate be-cause it may be when you're forced to sell for cash-flow rea-sons), what sense does it make to diversify?

Of course, diversifying across US-based stocks, US bonds, and US Treasury securities does nothing to minimize your exposure to the dollar and its potential weakening. All these assets are dollar denominated, so you will suffer real losses in purchasing power as the dollar declines relative to commod-ity prices and relative to other currencies of the world.

If you think you can minimize this by holding assets in all the countries of the world, good luck. There is no way you can become an expert in the economies of all the countries of the world, much less all their companies and all their finan-cial products. What exactly do you—or does anyone—know about adjustable-rate mortgages on condominiums in Spain financed by Italian banks?

And this leads to the next major weakness of diversification. Because you hold so many assets, you can't possibly evaluate their true value, so you use lots of middlemen such as financial advisers and stockbrokers to advise you. Right off the bat they cost you a percentage, quite possibly negating any benefit of diversification—and if they are unscrupulous and unethical, they could cost you much more than that.

Even if they are ethical, their motivations are simply different from yours. They don't really care if you lose half your net worth. They're getting paid whether you make money or not. Even hedge fund managers, who take 20 percent of the profits they generate for you and thus might seem more inclined to work scrupulously for you, are so highly leveraged with other people's money that it still pays for them to make enormous bets because if they score they can make as much as $5 billion a year, as John Paulson did in 2010. Once you make $5 billion in one year, it's tough to worry about the future value of the portfolio. The potential to make such large amounts of money in a single windfall or bonus makes for very short-term thinking.

Financial middlemen's incentives are different from the investors' in one important way. Yes, you want to maximize your returns, but you also want to minimize the risk of losing your principal. Think of how these financial advisers' business models work. Look at the individuals who provide financial advice to big investment entities like pension funds and insurance companies. Purchasing debt is still a rather mundane business, although junk bonds and vulture funds that invest in troubled, near bankrupt companies have made it a bit more exciting. But when a pension fund goes to interview a financial adviser or money manager in an attempt to hire someone to maximize its returns in its debt portfolio, the variability in historical performance across all the financial advisers available is very small.

Assume a market-based corporate bond debt portfolio today yields 4.5 percent and that most financial advisers recommend that you be well diversified. So if all bond funds are diversified, they will hold all corporate bonds. But all financial advisers' historical performance will reflect the market, and they'll be generating 4.5 percent returns. This isn't going to get them any business. If a few financial advisers or money managers can somehow consistently generate an additional ten basis points, they will garner all the investment dollars from almost all pension funds and insurance companies. They will top the rankings, year in and year out, at 4.6 percent while all the other financial middlemen generate 4.5 percent returns.

But what does efficient-market theory say about how these few generate the extra ten basis points? Theory says they have to take on more risk to do so. Maybe they are less diversified, maybe their portfolios hold a greater percentage of riskier bonds, or maybe they incorporate leverage in their investment philosophy, thus adding increased variability to the returns in the portfolio. The extra ten basis points of return are now sacrosanct to them because these points generate a huge flow of funds into their money management firms. They have to take on more risk to keep it up.

Like the earlier example of the banks having to match the aggressive, stupid lending of a dumb lender like Countrywide, here other bond funds look around, see they are losing customers and market share, and decide to do something about it. They too have to find a way to garner at least ten more basis points. And if they want to move to the top of the rankings, they better find a way to generate 15 to 20 basis points of unusual returns. Again, there's no easy way to do this in a sophisticated market without taking on more risk. All the competitors in this race of middlemen end up taking on more financial risk and passing it on to your portfolio.

What happens is that those financial managers who take on the most risk and do the stupidest type of nondiversified investing end up garnering the most clients and the most investment fees and become the richest in the sector. Your portfolio, run by these fund managers, is constantly being put into riskier and riskier investments using greater and greater leverage. This translates into greater fees for those money managers who promote it, but the risk of insolvency lies squarely on the principal investor such as the pension fund or the insurance company.

This ever-escalating competition in specialized markets is what drives bankers to make stupider and stupider loans with looser and looser terms and covenants. It is what drives equity and debt financial middlemen to recommend to their clients that they take on additional risk. It is what motivates money market funds to stretch for yield. This competition is clearly not understood by economists around the world. Economists like to think that in a competitive environment, those giving the best advice will succeed. This is clearly not the case. In the real world, those giving the worst advice garner the most clients and the greatest profits.

So a basic tenet of modern finance—that diversification is good—has proved false in the real world. This is revolutionary because diversification is the basis of almost all modern financial thinking. You cannot have a capital asset pricing model and portfolio theory and beta as a a measure of risk without the assumption that diversification is good.

The biggest cost of diversification may be a broad social cost because it can lead to managements of companies being poorly supervised by the very shareholders they are employed by. Even if you believe that, theoretically, the science is pure, in the world in which we live, where we rely on corrupt and unethical middlemen to advise us on portfolios constructed of thousands of different assets in hundreds of different countries around the world, it's nowhere near worth the risk.

TWELVE

REAL ASSETS—
REAL RETURNS

I hope I've convinced you by now that traditional investments are not going to do well in the troubled, corrupt, recessionary global environment we are facing. Unfortunately, although we are now heading into our sixth year of the global financial crisis, the end is nowhere in sight. With the entire world overleveraged, the world's largest countries at risk of defaulting on their debt, their most productive baby-boom citizens retiring, and their workforces aging and needing expensive medical care and retirement dollars, global demand looks to be precarious at best for a long time.

So if traditional investments don't work, where can people put their money to protect their principal and earn a reasonable return? You have to understand that in this type of environment, a reasonable real return is one in the low single digits. More important is to protect your principal from unexpected losses and to avoid losing more than half your purchasing power by dealing properly with inflation in the future.

I think it is time for smart investors to move from securities, stocks, and bonds into real assets. By real assets I mean gold and other commodities: land, houses, office buildings, apartment buildings, and even small businesses. There are many advantages in moving your assets from financial securities to real assets.

First, by focusing on the purchase of real assets, you'll free yourself (to a great degree) from dependence on corrupt bankers and self-interested stockbrokers and financial advisers. It's difficult to play in the financial asset market without going through a financial adviser. The same is not true of the real asset business. You can manage your own real assets. If you are close to retirement, you shouldn't be thinking about investing your total net worth in tax-free municipal bonds, which are subject to possible default and are a poor hedge against inflation, but rather about developing a second career or managing real properties around the country. This way you avoid Wall Street altogether.

It makes no sense to spend your productive time analyzing stocks and bonds. The reason is that, regardless of how much time and effort you expend, you can never match the effort of the thousands of Wall Street analysts and traders who do this full time. Pick any stock that you think you know a great deal about, and I can assure you there are literally hundreds of professional analysts who spend all their working hours researching that company and its earnings prospects.

What makes the game particularly unfair is that your analysis depends on publicly available information, whereas professionals on Wall Street do not limit themselves to that. Research analysts regularly call in to companies and insist on talking to the CFOs or CEOs to badger them to look at the analysts' projections for the companies' earnings, until the CEOs or CFOs agree that the analysts' estimates are either right on or too high or too low.

It would be funny if it weren't so illegal. A research analyst will call a CFO and say that she's prepared a 30-page spreadsheet on the company, and by her analysis it looks like next year's earnings will be $3.02 a share. And then she waits for the CFO to react. If the CFO doesn't react, the research analyst isn't shy. She says, "Do you think I'm being overly aggressive at $3.02, or do you think that there are other opportunities I haven't properly evaluated in my analysis that would make the earnings larger?" As long as she can keep the CFO on the phone, even a well-intentioned CFO will slowly leak information about the company's prospects and eventually signal what the company's earnings are going to be for the next quarter and the next year, if for no other reason than to get off the phone. So, if you're going up against the professionals who are playing with tomorrow's news today, you really have no chance.

It would be much better to invest your valuable time in a productive capacity. With real assets you can spend it investigating real properties and making determinations as to their attractiveness and potential returns. Once you acquire real properties, if you choose to, you can get into the asset management business and make a career out of visiting your properties and managing your tenants well to make sure you are maximizing your return. But the big advantage of real assets over financial assets is how they perform relative to inflation. Traditional financial assets like stocks, bonds, and Treasury bonds do poorly relative to inflation. Long-term bonds, as you can imagine, do the worst because they have a fixed return, which by definition cannot keep up with an unexpected inflation and the higher interest rates that result. As interest rates go up in the future, reflecting investors' demand that they protect their purchasing power, anybody who holds a fixed-income security is going to lose money.

Surprisingly, common stocks do very poorly with regard to unexpected inflation. I say surprisingly because, when you buy a common stock, you're supposed to be buying a percentage of a real company with real factories and real offices and bricks and mortar. And you would think that these real properties themselves would appreciate in an inflationary environment. Instead, in an inflationary environment, common stocks do poorly because interest rates are so high that the housing industry, automobile industry, and general economy all suffer. In a recession caused by high inflation and high interest rates, company earnings and company growth prospects evaporate, and stocks trade off significantly in price.

Treasury bonds, especially long-term Treasury bonds, are nothing but another form of fixed-income security, so they also do terribly relative to unexpected inflation. As I have discussed throughout this book, it is crucial that your investment portfolio perform well relative to inflation. That is because everything we know about the advanced countries of the world tells us that they are in recession, they face enormous operating deficits, and they are about to tap out on their ability to issue securities and borrow to fund their deficits. This means they have only two options: default or print money and cause inflation. And almost without exception, they will choose to print money rather than announce a formal default. So inflation is inevitable. As a matter of fact, I believe it's already here.

I am developing a theory that tries to explain how Ben Bernanke could triple the amount of currency and excess reserves in the system yet avoid an explosion of prices and wages. My theory starts with the question of what prices would be doing if Bernanke weren't printing money. Clearly we would have much greater deflation in wages and prices of goods. So just because prices aren't increasing, it doesn't mean there's a lack of inflation; rather, I would argue that Bernanke's printing of money is preventing deflation. Negative deflation equals inflation.

The Federal Reserve is rapidly printing money and causing currency levels to expand, thus wiping out that deflation. Prices look stable, but in real terms they're declining while the Federal Reserve masks this decline with massive increases in currency. So when someone asks you when inflation is coming back, I would argue it's already here.

You can see the effects of inflation already in the value of the dollar relative to stable currencies like the Japanese yen or the Norwegian kroner. Again, the dollar's weakness is masked when you compare it with traditional currencies like the euro or the Swiss franc because the European Union and Switzerland are also printing enormous amounts of currencies and inflating their currencies. It's as if countries are having a race to the bottom, yet the currency exchange rate between countries remains relatively stable because they're all making the same errors.

But relative to countries that so far have decided not to print additional currency, the US dollar has declined dramatically—about 35 or 40 percent against the yen and 29 percent relative to a basket of world currencies. This means the dollars have less purchasing power for imports or local goods in other countries.

More evident than even currency exchange rates is what has happened to the dollar's purchasing power relative to gold. As I said earlier, one dollar today buys only one-fiftieth the amount of gold it used to. Over the last 52 years, the dollar has devalued relative to gold by 98 percent—appropriately, I think. Gold itself hasn't changed much in true value or the amount of other assets like oil or silver you could buy with an ounce of gold because there is a large world reserve of it and little new mining. It is a very stable currency, unlike the dollar, which has seen enormous explosions of printing over the years as the US government tries to counterfeit money to fund its deficits.

There are financial securities that attempt to address this problem of unexpected inflation. They are known as Treasury Inflation-Protected Securities (TIPS). The way TIPS work is their current real yield is a market-determined yield, and at the end of each year, the government pays you not only this real yield but also an amount determined by however much the Consumer Price Index (CPI) has changed during that period. Thus, TIPS are supposed to automatically protect you against inflation by returning not just your principal amount but your principal amount adjusted for actual inflation.

Theoretically this sounds interesting, but there are a number of problems. First, again, you have to trust the government not to be corrupt. You have to trust it to compile CPI statistics correctly, which I don't believe the Bureau of Labor Statistics, which prepares the CPI, is doing. The CPI certainly doesn't properly measure the increasing costs of homes and college tuition and health-care expenditures properly, and it now allows for substituting goods, which takes out higher priced items and puts in lower priced items because economists argue that's what a rational person would do. But when you think about it, this drives down the reported level of inflation because you're removing from the basket of goods exactly those products and services that have increased in price the most.

Worse, the administrators who run the TIPS program may someday realize that if inflation dramatically increases interest rates, they won't be able to afford to pay out the promised returns. We're talking about a very large government that continually breaks its own rules and then sheepishly faults investors for trusting it. There's no guarantee that the US government won't change its own rules about how TIPS holders are compensated for inflation in the future.

If you have any doubts that governments can change the rules midstream, you need look no further than what happened with the recent Greek restructuring. The European governments finally came around and admitted that some creditors had to take a 50 percent writeoff on their debt investments in Greece but somehow convinced themselves that this was voluntary, and therefore not a true default, so credit default swap (CDS) contracts sold to guarantee Greek debt to investors did not pay out. I can't think of a better definition of corruption.

In this and the last two chapters, I hope to convince you to move some of your assets to gold and other commodities, which requires caution. The easiest way to accomplish it is through exchange-traded funds (ETFs). But ETFs are also set up to disappoint. It turns out that commodity ETFs, like gold funds, are not even monitored or investigated by the Securities and Exchange Commission. Rather they are supposedly regulated and monitored by the Commodities Futures Trading Commission (CFTC).

I think this loose regulation might lead some ETF managers into unethical and possibly criminal activity because an ETF really is nothing more than an index that reflects the underlying commodity's price. If you run a gold ETF, you don't have to take the money you receive and buy gold. You can just report the gold price that you see in the newspaper every day as your asset value. It will be years before investors try to sell their ETF and find out there is no gold in it, that the managers had been stealing the proceeds à la Bernie Madoff, and they never had any intention of buying gold.

Many of the ETFs known as gold ETFs don't hold any gold at all. They just hold derivative positions that are supposed to, if the market cooperates, reflect the price of gold. Well, good luck with that. We've already seen that derivatives are enormously volatile and difficult to price and understand. Also, during periods of crises, their prices are unpredictable, and there is no way anybody can tell you that a complex derivative position is going to reflect an underlying commodity price. So if you invest in this type of gold ETF, gold may double in value, and the value of your derivative ETF position may decline.

Luckily the real value of investing in real assets is that they do keep up with general inflation. The same studies which found that financial assets such as stocks, bonds, and Treasuries do a poor job of keeping up with unanticipated inflation also found that commodities such as gold, homes, and office buildings, over a long period of time, typically do a very good job. It makes sense. If you're buying commodities or office buildings, you're literally buying bricks and mortar, which are material goods. And in a world of general inflation caused by too many dollars, those dollars cause all prices of all goods and all wages to increase commensurately.

If you hold physical assets, your assets should appreciate at the inflation rate. Not that you've made any real money. By earning the inflation rate on a gold investment, you're just maintaining your purchasing power. You haven't earned a single dollar of real return. So that is the trade-off with holding gold. By definition, it is unproductive. But because it is such an enormous store of wealth in the world and such a stable currency, it should do a good job protecting you against unanticipated inflation. So by holding gold, you're giving up the opportunity to earn real returns if the economy recovers (highly unlikely), but you're protecting yourself against inflation in the future. As I said, in this global environment, it seems silly to worry about real returns of 1 percent versus 2 percent when you could lose 50 percent of your purchasing power if inflation reignites. The real threat to your assets is not losing 1 percent per year in real terms; it's losing 50 percent because of not planning properly.

What's the best real asset to purchase right now? In 2009, my recommendation was to invest in gold. At the time, gold was trading for $700 an ounce, and I thought this was a fair price relative to how much I thought Bernanke was going to inflate the dollar. Gold eventually reached $1,950 a little more than two years later and has since settled at approximately $1,750 an ounce.

But at these levels, I feel uncomfortable telling people to put all their assets into gold. There is a great deal of speculative activity in gold, and while it's entirely possible we'll see a much weaker dollar over the next 15 to 20 years, and gold approaching $10,000 an ounce, in the short run there is nothing to keep gold from trading down to the $1,250 to $1,350 range. If you can stand such volatility in the short run, gold makes for a good long-term investment and hedge against inflation. But if you don't like the idea of losing another 25 percent of the market value of your assets, you probably don't want to put everything you own into gold right now.

Even though gold is stable in its purchasing power, in this world we still spend dollars as our prime currency. People don't buy things with gold, at least not yet (although I've read recently that some hotels now are accepting gold bullion as payment). Because you have to pay your expenses in dollars, you need your investment portfolio to eventually translate into dollars. If you hold all your assets in gold, you will always be subject to the vagaries of the dollar-gold exchange rate, which is volatile and may not reflect the true inherent value of gold minute to minute but rather the speculative activity of highly leveraged commodity hedge fund players.

The best real asset in this environment, I think, is your own home. To those of you who are still renting, I would recommend you go out and buy.

Why does home buying make sense now? Prices have dropped. Some California cities have seen average price declines of about 60 percent. Nationally the average home price has declined 24 to 32 percent in real terms.

Based on my analysis, then, the market should be bottoming out because prices have returned to 1997 levels, the levels before the bubble. The fluff is gone. New mortgage lending is much saner than the crazy amounts of money that were extended during the boom. Many cities are seeing homes trade at prices below what it would cost to build them today. If housing prices continue downward from their current levels, they would essentially be overreacting, trading below their fair long-term value. Again, you might have a short-term loss of 5 or 10 percent more if the economy still stays incredibly weak. But you should take comfort from the knowledge that at those levels, the values of the homes will be depressed relative to people's incomes and potential rental incomes, so over the long term they should trade back up to higher levels.

Even though we had a national crisis, housing is still a local market. You need to do a great deal of research on Zillow. com and other resources to make sure that your community's homes have adjusted properly downward in price during this recession. Surprisingly, the wealthiest areas of some of the richest cities in our country, which appreciated the most during the boom, still have not declined to their 1997 levels. I think the reason is that the rich in this country are still earning a significant percentage of total income and control the vast majority of wealth and assets in the country. In other words, recessions just don't hit rich people the same way they do middle-income people, and that was especially true this time.

In the wealthy enclave of Santa Barbara, prices have come down, but someone worth $30 million or $40 million really doesn't care if a house costs $3 million or $4 million, whereas in a more moderate-income California city like Riverside, the price drop has been more significant because moderate-income families barely have enough for the down payment and are dependent on the bank's lending rules and qualifying amounts to determine how much they are able to pay. If banks are willing to lend only four times your income today, whereas they once lent eight to ten times your income, you have to either make a large down payment or wait until prices come way down. That's what has happened in Riverside. The city has seen its median home price drop from close to $500,000 at its peak to $184,000 today.

So if you live in a wealthy area like Manhattan or Santa Monica or La Jolla, be careful. Prices still have not declined as much as they should. I'm not certain they ever will, but there is always a risk. It's normal for the richer neighborhoods to be the last to adjust to a housing-price decline because the rich have access to lots of other assets, in addition to income, to draw on in making their mortgage payments. The rich are not going to be forced into foreclosure by the banks. But if market values in these wealthy neighborhoods do eventually decline by 20 or 30 percent, it would be irrational for even a rich person to continue to pay the mortgage on a million-dollar house if the same house next door is selling for $800,000. A rational person would default on the mortgage and buy the same house across the street for a lot less money.

There's another reason that even wealthy enclaves are subject to the rules of economics. While we have a great number of enormously wealthy people in this country, we also have a large number of wannabes. You'd be surprised how many 30-something couples with a combined income of a couple hundred thousand dollars and less than $500,000 in the bank have two-million- and three-million- and four-million-dollar homes in an attempt to keep up with the Joneses or at least to give that appearance. These people are going to be financially squeezed. If they both still have their jobs, maybe they're getting by, but it will be difficult for them to continue to make mortgage payments that are such a large percentage of their take-home pay, especially as rates tick upward from the initial teaser rates they enjoyed on their adjustable-rate and option-pay mortgages. So even what appear to be wealthy enclaves are not completely safe from significant price drops.

But let's assume you've done your analysis, and in the community you want to live (or purchase investment properties), prices are 35 or 40 percent lower than they were five or six years ago, and it looks like prices in surrounding neighborhoods are stabilizing. In this case, buying a home might make a great deal of sense. And the reason is not obvious. I'm not predicting that home prices in real terms are going to jump in the future—just the opposite. I think they're going to stay relatively flat, and I would be surprised if you generated a real positive return on the house simply because there's just not going to be great demand for houses in the future.

Given the weak economy and the lack of good-paying job prospects here, legal immigration has slowed by some

60 percent and illegal immigration is off by some 80 percent. Many elderly people are leaving their homes and moving into assisted-living facilities and nursing homes. This puts a great surplus of homes on the market and should depress prices.

Finally, young people who had no problem investing more than 100 percent of their net worth in a house during the boom years, when prices were doubling every four years, now understand that trees do not grow to the sky. House prices can go down as well as up. Home prices are enormously volatile, especially when you adjust for the huge amount of debt leverage a home buyer typically employs through mortgage borrowing. And so there is no free lunch. Young couples used to put 55 or 60 percent of their take-home pay toward their mortgage payments, but I would be surprised if they were willing to do that in the future, now that they understand that housing is just like every other investment: It goes up and down. I would think that many young couples would choose to rent in the future, which is a rational thing to do. Why subject your family to the stresses of trying to make a mortgage payment that far exceeds your ability to pay?

There is obviously some inherent joy in owning your own home, but is it worth putting your family through that stress and spending so much on the mortgage that you can't enjoy vacations together, you can't afford a new car? You can barely afford nights out at restaurants and movies once a month. And you would never save enough money after your mortgage payments to be able to start your own business and free yourself from your corporate cubicle. No, I think people will start acting a lot more rationally, as I see no reason that young people shouldn't rent in this environment rather than own.

So if houses are not going to appreciate wildly in real terms, why am I recommending you buy a house? The major reason is that home prices, while not appreciating in real terms, historically have done a good job of appreciating with inflation in nominal terms. In other words, historically homes have been a wonderful hedge against unanticipated inflation. If inflation reignites to 10 to 12 percent a year, and stocks decline and bonds collapse, historically it has been true that houses appreciate at almost exactly the rate of inflation rate—in this example, 10 to 12 percent. By holding the house, even on an unleveraged basis with no mortgage debt, you protect your purchasing power, which has to be your objective as an investor, given the outlook for global inflation and higher interest rates.

But the real beauty of buying a home is not on the asset side of your balance sheet; it is on the liability side of your balance sheet. The last great financial opportunity in the world for consumers is available right now for home buyers, and that is the ability to borrow at a low fixed rate for 30 years. Businesses can't do it. Property developers can't do it. Unsecured borrowers can't do it. The only people who can get 30-year, fixed-rate money are home buyers. And the 30-year time frame is important because, although I am certain inflation and interest rates will increase in the future, there is no telling when it will happen. It may happen this year. It may happen in three years. But it wouldn't surprise me if it took five to eight years for investors to finally realize that the United States is in financial difficulty. If you had borrowed money for only ten years, and interest rates started exploding because of inflation in the seventh year of your mortgage, you wouldn't have any windfall on the monies you borrowed. What you want to have is debt outstanding for a long maturity after inflation pushes up interest rates in the future. This is where homeownership can be a real investing home run.

If you lock in interest rates now at 4 percent and buy a home, your neighbors will be incredibly jealous five to seven years from now when you're paying 4 percent, and they are forced to borrow at 10 or 12 percent. This means the true carrying value of your debt in real terms, because it is fixed-rate debt, will have declined by more than half. So investors can make money not just by buying assets that increase in value; they also can make money by borrowing money on a fixed-rate basis in an inflationary environment and have that debt in real terms decrease in value. Like I said before, if you expect inflation to come back, you don't want to be an investor in fixed-return assets; you want to be a borrower. You want to be able to pay back your creditors with deflated dollars that are easier to earn in that environment.

Not only are the government and banks continuing to offer homeowners 30-year loans at a fixed rate, but they're doing it on bargain terms. The Federal Reserve continues to hold down interest rates in an attempt to heal the banks, but this provides an enormous opportunity for borrowers. To say that the US Treasury's ability to borrow 30-year money at 3 percent is a good deal for the Treasury or a 30-year bank loan to buy a home at 4 percent money is a steal are understatements. Think about it. How could one individual with one job that he might lose tomorrow be such a good credit risk that someone would be willing to lend him money at 4 percent a year? Heck, Spain and Italy have to pay 6 or 7 percent per year to borrow money. Are you a better credit risk than Spain or Italy? Don't answer that.

So the timing from an interest-rate perspective is perfect. I don't care whether interest rates in the future go from 4 percent for 30-year, fixed-rate mortgages down to 3.875 percent or even to 3.75 percent. I'm not trying to calculate the absolute peak of this bubble. I just know that interest rates are lower than they should be, that Treasury securities are in an enormous bubble of value because of these low interest rates, and that homeowners can enjoy below-market pricing for their interest rate if they lock in fixed-rate financing for 30 years. I think you'll look like a genius if you either refinance your home today at 4 percent or go out and buy a home under those terms.

Because you can use enormous leverage in the purchase of a home (again, where else can you borrow five or six times your income to make an asset purchase?), the potential returns to you as a homeowner are tremendous. Even though your home may not appreciate a single dollar in real terms, if it just keeps up with inflation and your debt costs are fixed, then simple arithmetic says that your equity investment will explode. Here's a simple example. You buy a home today for $500,000, and its value does nothing more than keep up with inflation, assumed to be 4.5 percent per year in this example. In 20 years you can sell it for $1.2 million, and your debt will have declined from $400,000 (you had to put 20 percent, or $100,000, down) to approximately $200,000. Your equity, meanwhile, will have increased from $100,000 to $1 million. Where else are you going to see a tenfold return on an investment? And because of leverage and your fixed debt costs, this is not just keeping up with inflation. It probably would take $200,000 or $220,000 to buy items that were worth $100,000 twenty years earlier, but the remaining accretion of your equity to $1 million is all real profit.

I don't know of any other investment opportunity like this for individuals today. That you can walk away if things go bad and leave the house with the bank is just another fringe benefit. And if we are wrong and mortgage interest rates do decline to 3 percent, which would be incredible, you can always re-finance for free with few closing costs. So I don't see any real downside to this, and the upside is enormous. You may find it funny that the person who wrote books predicting the housing crash is now suggesting that the best investment he knows is to buy a home with long-term, fixed-rate debt. I'm nothing if not flexible!

THIRTEEN

GOLD AS A YARDSTICK AND AS AN INVESTMENT

The investment allocation decision is a very personal decision subject to your particular circumstances. That is why, in addition to writing books for the general public, I also offer a personalized one-on-one financial consulting service to individuals and families at my website, www.stopthelying.com. Through an extended series of emails and phone conversations, I can become familiar with the financial issues facing you and your family and begin to figure out the appropriate direction to take your investment strategy.

In 2009, in my book *Contagion*, I recommended that my readers move a substantial amount of their assets from traditional investments like stocks, bonds, government securities, and money markets into gold. At the time gold was at $700, and it eventually reached $1,950.

Because gold is trading today at $1,750 an ounce, it is difficult to recommend that people put a substantial percentage of their total assets into one asset, gold. But I still firmly believe that gold is the best real asset to hold over the long term to protect yourself from unexpected inflation, and in this chapter I'll explain why. It may sound radical to suggest you hold 25 to 35 percent of your assets in gold. But think about it. Right now you're probably holding 100 percent of your assets in dollar-denominated securities. You have to ask yourself which is the better long-term receptacle for wealth—the US dollar or gold. Historically gold has been much more stable than the dollar, which is not only extremely volatile but has declined dramatically in value over time.

Figure 1 shows the value of an ounce of gold priced in US dollars. Clearly gold has appreciated dramatically over time. But the easiest way to see how far the dollar has fallen in purchasing power is to not think of how many dollars it costs to buy an ounce of gold but of how many ounces of gold it takes to buy a dollar. It sounds simple enough, but because we have

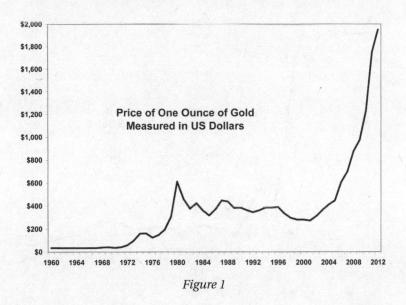

Figure 1

grown up pricing everything in dollars, it can actually be quite difficult to recalibrate how you measure value.

Figure 2 shows what has happened to the value of the dollar as measured in ounces of gold. As you can see, over time the real value of a dollar has collapsed relative to the more stable currency, gold. In fact, relative to gold, the US dollar has lost more than 98 percent of its purchasing power in the last 52 years. Its biggest decline happened in the 1970s, when the government took us off the gold standard and began rapidly printing dollars to fund its large deficits, and the next biggest decline began in 2001.

If gold is a much better yardstick of value than the dollar, plotting asset values over time in gold ounces should produce a historical graph that makes a lot more sense to us. Figure

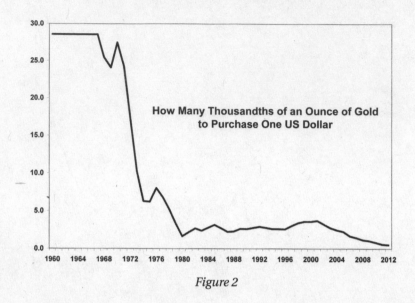

Figure 2

3 is a historical picture of the Dow Jones Industrial Average, priced in dollars. This is the traditional way of looking at the value of the stock market, by measuring it in dollars. Through this lens, you can see why investors and politicians feel pretty good about the direction of the Dow and the economy.

But because the dollar's value is so variable and has declined so dramatically over time, it makes no sense to try to make statements about whether the stock market is going up or down when we value it in dollars. It is as if we used a yardstick to measure the width of a room, but the yardstick not only shrinks over time but varies greatly in length from week to week.

It may sound strange to question measuring things in dollars when the dollar is still the standard measurement of

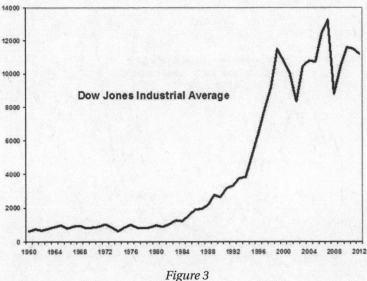

Figure 3

value, but it does lead to a lot of erroneous conclusions. Just look at Figure 3. You can see, for instance, that the government stimulus program in 2009 and 2010 appeared to have a positive effect on the stock market, giving people hope that the stimulus would create jobs and pull us out of a recession. The stock market is a good predictor of future economic activity because it is a look at a company's future earnings. So it's understandable that one might look at this graph and see the beginnings of recovery, but this is a mirage. Figure 3 is misleading because it measures the value of stocks in dollars, and the dollar itself is dramatically declining in value during this same period.

Figure 4 shows the Dow Jones Industrial Average over the same time period but priced in ounces of gold instead of

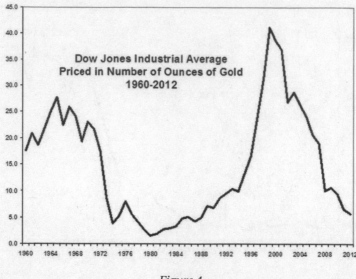

Figure 4

dollars. Now, because gold is a much more stable currency and measure of wealth than the dollar, we get a dramatically different and much more accurate picture of what has happened to the Dow Jones Industrial Average over time. No longer are investors getting richer every day—quite the contrary.

The graph shows that the postwar period was one of growth until the 1970s. Then, with the printing of currency by the Fed, the wealth of stock investors dropped precipitously for two reasons. The printing of currency made the dollar worth a lot less, and the inflation that resulted caused a severe recession as home building and autos cratered because of high interest rates.

The economy lags until the election of Ronald Reagan, but it was not his tax cuts or tax increases that caused growth in the stock market and wealth to take off; it was that Paul Volker and the Fed stopped printing money. It takes a while for people to believe that the money spigot has been turned off permanently, but over the next 20 years, interest rates declined and the economy exploded. Unfortunately, because of the high-tech bubble, the economy and the stock market became overheated during Bill Clinton's second term, from 1996 to 2000.

But after the election of George W. Bush in 2000, the trend is unmistakable: down, down, down. And fast. In the 12 years after George W. Bush was elected, the stock market lost 90 percent of its purchasing power relative to gold. (Investors have done slightly better than Figure 4 suggests, as they were receiving some small dividends during this period, which this graph does not reflect, but the overall shape of the graph is still the same.)

The decline in the Dow was caused by the largest recession/depression since the Great Depression, the bursting of both the hi-tech and housing bubbles, and Ben Bernanke's reaction, which was to print more currency at the Fed. The ineffectiveness of such currency inflation could not be clearer.

By thinking of the Dow's value in terms of dollars (Figure 3), we patted ourselves on the back for years, in the belief that we grew richer and richer as our stock market increased in value. Now it is obvious that we are much poorer than we were years ago. Specifically, in 2009 and 2010, when the government was promoting a big stimulus to help us pull out of the recession, the stimulus did no such thing. Yes, the stock market measured in dollars increased temporarily, but when you look at the Dow's value in terms of the much more stable gold ounces, you can see that the market was not fooled at all by this stimulus program.

Figure 5 shows the Dow average for the period from 1992 to 2012. Pricing the Dow in gold ounces reveals the stimulus plans of 2008 to 2010 for exactly what they were—just a shuffling of paper with no real economic wealth effect, certainly no positive one. We can argue whether the stimulus money was completely wasted, but it almost never makes sense to try to stimulate an economy by borrowing from one person and letting the government spend that money, knowing it has to

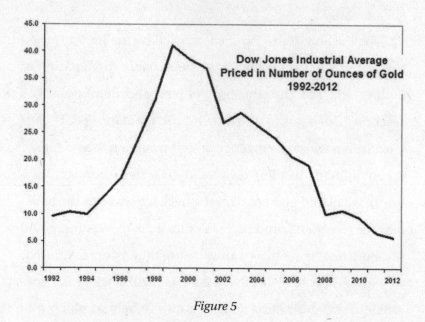

Figure 5

repay it in the future. If consumption is greater today, it must eventually be less, when the piper must be repaid.

Note that I have plotted the Dow instead of GDP in making these pronouncements about the effect of the stimulus on country wealth. Some might want to see a graph of GDP priced in gold ounces to see what effects the printing of money has on GDP. But I don't think this is mathematically valid. GDP is an annual flow, not a measure of wealth or an asset with a long life, so it would be unfair to apply the price of gold to it as a deflator because the market price of gold captures not only historical and current inflation but also investors' best estimate of future inflation. If you want to deflate nominal prices by measuring things in gold ounces, it is only fair to apply this method to stores of wealth like the Dow and Standard & Poor's 500, country currencies, or assets of very long life such as copper, silver, and platinum.

I understand how difficult this very simple concept of pricing things in gold rather than in dollars is to grasp because I've been wrestling with it myself for three years now. Who would think that just simply inverting the price of gold measured in dollars and instead talking about the value of a dollar measured in a currency called ounces of gold would be so confusing? But it really is. We have lived our whole lives pricing things in dollars and thinking of dollars as constant yardsticks. We have to get out of that habit. I suggest we begin to price a lot of assets in ounces of gold. Now, you can't price everything in gold ounces. It doesn't make any sense to look at the minimum wage, for example, over time priced in gold ounces. The reason illuminates why gold is such a wonderful hedge against inflation. The minimum wage is not an asset with a long-term life; it is a momentary snapshot of the level of wages we offer our poorest citizens. Therefore, it is inappropriate to look at an operating expense or annual expense like the minimum wage and discount it or price it in ounces of gold. Gold is a long-term asset and incorporated in its price is everybody's future expectation of inflation. If you receive a minimum-wage payment of seven dollars an hour, you actually get the seven dollars today. To say that you get so many ounces of gold today is not a fair comparison because that gold price measured in dollars incorporates high expectations of inflation in the future, which have no bearing on the seven dollars you receive immediately.

So valuing things in terms of gold ounces is useful and important, but doing so should be limited to those assets that have very long lives. Luckily there are lots of those. And when you plot their values, the historical graph tells fascinating stories.

Figure 6 shows the average value of a home in the United States priced in dollars. As you can see, many people believed that the prices of homes in dollars had appreciated for about 50 years running, so they were surprised when prices started dropping in 2006.

But is this really what happened?

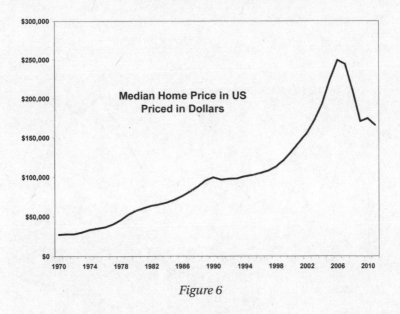

Figure 6

Figure 7 shows the same graph of house prices but in gold ounces, not dollars. It provides the basis for a proper analysis of historical home prices. No, they haven't been growing nonstop for decades. They have moved dramatically up and down in price. As interest rates moved up in the 1970s, home prices, valued in gold ounces, did come down. Although interest rates were increasing only nominally and not on a real basis, these higher nominal interest rates caused the banks to lend less to home buyers, and thus prices came down. Nominal interest rates are simply the real rate of return a lender demands given the risks of the loan plus the expected inflation rate.

As interest rates started declining in 1980, home prices increased. But that all changed in 2005–2006 with the housing

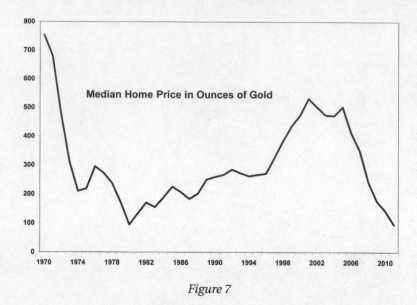

Figure 7

crash. Now prices of homes measured in gold ounces look so low as to be a bargain, another reason I am recommending moving into hard assets like homes instead of financial securities.

Figure 8 shows the number of ounces of silver it takes to buy one ounce of gold historically. The shape of the graph mostly reflects the scarcity of silver and new methods to mine it, but I did want to show that by taking the US dollar out of the equation, we can now compare the relative values of two commodities without the debilitating effects of trying to measure things in dollars.

You can see that the exchange rate between silver and gold is much less volatile than you would think. The reason is that

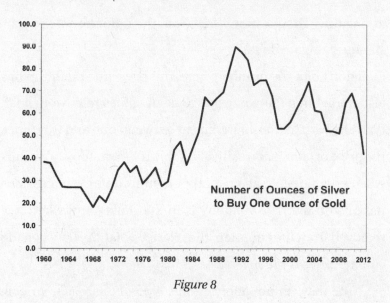

Number of Ounces of Silver
to Buy One Ounce of Gold

Figure 8

you're used to measuring gold and silver in dollars, and we know the dollar itself adds tremendous volatility to the story.

We can safely conclude that gold is indeed a stable yardstick and storer of wealth because it has a narrow band of value relative to other long-term commodity assets. Of course the relationship does have some variation over time because silver has productive uses, and varying deposits of silver are constantly being explored and discovered. So the reserves of silver, and the supply and demand for silver, are constantly changing.

The only open question in the graph is why silver became worth less relative to gold in the 1980s. Offhand I don't know the answer, but for the first time, I feel like we are at least asking the right questions, free from the influence of the constantly changing dollar.

I don't plot the numbers here, but over time platinum has also traded in a fairly narrow range of values relative to gold, typically with platinum trading at between one and two times the price of gold. This relatively stable relationship also results when you plot gold against other commodities, such as copper or iron ore. The volatility is in the dollar, and when it is removed from the equation, the relative volatility between the commodities is much less.

Note that I'm not applying this type of analysis to pricing short-term assets, such as oil or pork bellies. I don't think this is appropriate because, as I said, gold is a long-term asset, which in its price has captured not just this year's expected inflation rate but the inflation rate for all time into the future. So if you have a commodity like oil in a tanker (as opposed to oil in the ground), which typically gets consumed pretty quickly and is not stored for long periods of time, or you have an asset like pork bellies, which have a real shelf life and so cannot be stored for long periods of time, I don't think it's appropriate to look at their value in ounces of gold, but it's still important to recognize that when you do look at dollar price histories of these shorter-term assets, you're getting a lot of wrong information.

I hope you've found this analysis illuminating. Not only does it tell us a lot about the economic times in which we live, by giving a much clearer picture of home prices, stock prices, currencies, and long-term asset prices over time, but it should also convince you that you're making a terrible mistake by holding a substantial percentage of your investment portfolio in dollar-denominated assets. It is why I recommend that almost everyone hold some percentage of assets in gold.

As a matter of fact, I think even at $1,750 an ounce, if you were a very long-term investor with a 15- to 20-year investment horizon, you need to hold a fairly substantial percentage of your assets in gold and hard assets because I don't see any way the United States or, for that matter, other countries of the world can get out of their debt problems without inflating their currencies dramatically. As they inflate, their currencies will devalue relative to real assets, and the prices of these real assets will increase in nominal dollar terms but not in real terms. If you're locked into a fixed-return investment vehicle, or if you have lent money out and expect to get the principal returned in the future without an inflation adjustment, you could suffer tremendously.

I hate to even think it, but it's not impossible that gold could approach $10,000 an ounce over the next 15 to 20 years. Again, gold is not going to go up in real terms. Gold has no productive uses. Gold isn't going to be more valuable. It's the dollar that's going to collapse, so it will take more dollars to buy an ounce of gold. And to me it's not crazy to think the dollar could collapse in value another 80 percent because we have $3 trillion of currency and reserves outstanding, and the government has $14 trillion in debt, more than $20 trillion in unfunded liabilities in Social Security and Medicare, and future deficits that will push that debt up by more than a trillion dollars a year going forward.

If the United States has exhausted its borrowing authority, it will print money to fund these deficits. So the $3 trillion of currency and excess reserves outstanding could easily triple, quadruple, or quintuple. If it does, and Bernanke or his successor prints another $12 trillion of currency or extends that to the banks to make them whole on their bad loans, gold will probably appreciate four- or fivefold, and $10,000 an ounce is not an unrealistic price over a 20-year period.

So I conclude that not only is gold a much better yardstick and measure of wealth than the US dollar, but it's also a much better storer of wealth and a better investment than dollar-denominated assets. The government can turn on the printing presses and inflate the amount of dollars in the marketplace overnight. It's almost impossible to inflate the amount of gold in the system quickly. A huge amount of gold is stored in the federal reserves and central banks of the countries of the world relative to the amount of gold that is used in either productive capacities or is mined. It is this huge ratio of existing gold reserves relative to its uses or new mining finds that make gold an ideal currency.

Of course the one advantage of holding dollar-denominated assets versus gold is that today we still both value things in dollars and purchase things in dollars. It is our currency of choice. So when you invest in dollar-denominated assets and earn dollars, you use those dollars to make purchases in the real economy. Especially for short-term investors, this eliminates the risk of investing in gold and having to convert into dollars before you can make a purchase in the real economy.

If businesses accepted ounces of gold as payment for hotel rooms and meals at French restaurants, this problem would be eliminated, and I would feel much more comfortable in recommending a higher percentage of your assets be held in gold. But that day will not be upon us soon. I don't envision a day when people will vacate the dollar and prevent its use as a currency, but the government will so inflate it that you will be glad you're holding a hard asset like gold.

I think people's biggest concern now about holding gold is whether they're too late. Has gold already made its move? Is gold now a new bubble? I think not. Once you start to understand that you need to price dollars in gold ounces rather than gold ounces in dollars, you'll see it's the dollar that's devaluing, not gold that's increasing in real value or creating a bubble. Gold is not in a bubble at these price levels. Its price solely reflects the enormous amount of dollar printing that Bernanke has done and the devaluation of the dollar.

But the price of gold also tries to incorporate people's expectations of future inflation, and I don't think anybody thinks that Bernanke is done printing money. To date his printing has gone to fund the bad loan losses that banks have in the mortgage market, but the banks still have enormous amounts of bad loans that they have not recognized on their books, and the sovereign debt crisis of European countries and Japan is just starting. And, as I said, the amount of sovereign debt on the banks' books dwarfs the amount of bad mortgage loans they held by a factor of eight to ten. So Bernanke is going to have lots of sick banks that need saving in the future, and you can be sure he'll be turning on the presses to aid his friends.

As I discussed in the early chapters of this book, all the countries of the world are in serious financial trouble, with too much debt and large operating deficits in the middle of a global recession, with huge numbers of seniors retiring and losing their productive capacity. This tells you that the operating deficits of these governments will continue for some time into the future, especially in the United States, where the populace is so antitax and liberal economists are promoting additional spending in a wrongheaded effort to generate jobs. Our policies are all wrong with regard to government deficits. We are overleveraged, and our government is so broken and controlled by big campaign contributions from banks and big corporations, there is little hope that we will end up doing the smart thing with regard to our deficits and debt over time. We will just stumble along and continue devaluing our currency.

As an investor, you will wish that you held a percentage of your assets in gold.

To demonstrate the power of holding gold as an investment, let's look at a hypothetical. If you had invested all your assets in gold in 1990, you would have outperformed all other mutual funds, bond funds, and even almost all hedge funds over the period, even those that reported nominal returns in excess of 8 percent per year. We are being fooled by these financial advisers and fund managers who report their performance in dollars. When properly measured in gold ounces, much of their superior performance disappears.

If you needed any more proof of the mistakes that economists make in analyzing global economics, because of their inability to get a handle on this varying measure of wealth that is the US dollar, in 2011, Bernanke announced that he was thinking about extending his quantitative easing programs into the future, which were his plans to print more money and buy more bonds. The stock market went up 1 percent on this announcement, measured in dollars of course, and everybody—*Wall Street Journal, New York Times,* CNBC, and others—said it was obvious that the stock market loved the idea of additional quantitative easing. Well, you can't have quantitative easing without Bernanke's printing more dollars, and you don't see that by looking at the stock market's reaction measured in dollars.

On the same day as Bernanke's announcement, it turns out, gold went up 5 percent in value measured in dollars. So think what actually happened. The stock market went up 1 percent, but gold went up 5 percent. So in real terms, measured in ounces of gold, the stock market went down 4 percent. The market didn't like Ben's idea at all.

If people actually measured the stock market that way, editors would have written completely different headlines for stories about Bernanke's announcement. I can see the headlines now: "Stock market drops 4 percent on Bernanke's announcement of additional quantitative easing as measured in ounces of gold." The stock market hated the idea of Bernanke doing additional quantitative easing.

It's incredible to me that a basic fact, such as whether the stock market has increased or decreased based on an announcement of new information, is so obscured. How can we expect economists to get things right in the long term when they don't even know the direction the stock market is going on a particular day? If you look back, each time Ben Bernanke has announced that he plans to do more quantitative easing, the dollar has devalued such that even if the stock market appeared to rally in dollar terms, in real terms it actually declined.

Start thinking about measuring things in ounces of gold, and you will get a much clearer picture of both the economy and your own financial position. It would be a helpful exercise for you to measure your total assets over time in dollars and then do a comparable analysis in ounces of gold. It may be discouraging, as few of you will have seen significant appreciations in your net worth. But you can change that by refocusing your portfolio on real assets, especially some percentage invested in gold. You will protect the value of your portfolio and preserve the purchasing power of your assets in the dangerous world of unanticipated inflation.

FOURTEEN

A BRAVE NEW WORLD

I've covered a great deal of ground in this book. I started with a day at the races and showed that even small horse tracks around the country are more ethically and less criminally organized than our largest and most sophisticated financial markets and our government. I examined in detail the corruption throughout our banking system, including why the bankers themselves are writing the laws.

I discussed the economic future of the United States to see how much trouble its rising debt levels and annual deficits will cause. I suggested why it is foolish for journalists and pundits to conclude that because the United States has been a large, well-financed, and safe place to put money in the past, it will automatically continue to be so in the future. This is the same logic that said because home prices went up 50 years in a row that they would have to continue to go up for 10 or 20 more. There's no guarantee that the United States will always be a world power, that its currency will be strong, or that its debts will be safely repaid. It would be a disaster for the global economic environment if the United States failed to repay its debts, but nothing is impossible. If you look at just the sheer magnitude of the numbers, you begin to understand how difficult it will be for the United States to clean up its debt.

As I discussed, the situation is further complicated by the retirement of the baby boomers. We're losing their productivity and absorbing the costs of their retirement and health care, and at the same time we are going through the worst global recession in 70 years. This is a recipe for disaster, especially because we're entering this period with record debts and record deficits. I don't know how high debt has to get in the United States as a percentage of GDP to begin to scare people, but at 100 percent today, and forecast to quickly reach 140 percent of GDP, it certainly seems like time to sweat. We can argue which is the most egregious violation of ethics by our government, but to me it is a simple choice. All the small-time bribe taking and pandering for votes by our members of Congress is dwarfed by the license that our Federal Reserve, owned and controlled by our nation's banks, has to print money, devalue our currency, and give that money to the banks to make them whole on their bad loans. Nothing is as destructive to a global economy as the inflation that printing money causes.

What's most disturbing about the current crisis is that it's not just limited to the United States. Almost every advanced country of the world is in crisis. People don't even mention Japan these days because its economy is flat on its back. But as I said earlier, Japan has 230 percent debt to GDP. Remember, any country with more than 60 percent debt to GDP is in danger of going into default. How Japan is holding this together and borrowing at record-low rates is astounding—but it won't go on forever.

Europe is a complete mess. It's not just Portugal, Ireland, Italy, Greece, and Spain, although they're all in enormous trouble; it's that the UK, France, and Germany are already leveraged with debt equal to 80 percent of their GDP, and they haven't even started bailing out their own bad banks, which are sitting on enormous amounts of foreign lending to Portugal, Ireland, Italy, Greece, and Spain and their banks.

There's no easy way for Europe to get out of this mess. Europe thinks it can just have the International Monetary Fund and the European Central Bank provide bailouts, and get the Germans and French to issue loan guarantees, and everything will just go away, as if by providing a guarantee, bad loans somehow become good. Bad loans are bad because the underlying entity doesn't have any money to pay interest and principal. A guarantee does nothing to improve that cash-flow position. It just shifts the liability to a different party.

The way to help Greece is to forgive their debt, not lend Greek institutions more monies. Now that Greece has announced that it may default on 50 percent of its debts, and Greece is a very small country, it's not clear where this stops. As each country defaults, global banks have more losses that need to be bailed out. Governments today seem more intent on taking care of bank creditors than their own citizens.

I also pointed out that no reform is coming. We've been in crisis for five years now, and the most brilliant things to come out of Washington, DC, are the Democrats' plan to cut deficits by spending more government money, and the Republicans' plan to cut deficits by cutting taxes on the wealthy. As I said, it would be laughable if it didn't cause so much pain to so many millions around the world. No. There can be no true reform in the economics sphere until we reform our system of money and politics, until we outlaw lobbyists.

President Obama made this mistake with his health-care bill. He thought he would pass health-care reform first and worry about dealing with lobbyists later. Well, his health-care bill got captured by the lobbyists and never emerged again. The insurance companies, the HMOs, the hospital corporations, and the pharmaceutical companies wrote the legislation that Republicans have so derisively dubbed Obamacare, and it preserved their status quo—the cost inefficiencies of the old health-care system, destroying any chance that Americans would see a reduction of health-care costs in the future. We can't go on like this. The first step in any reforms in banking, environmental laws, health-care financing, and the provision of insurance, global warming, education, and criminal justice must be lobbying reform. Until we get the money out of Washington, big banks and big corporations will be calling all the shots in Washington and writing legislation to preserve their power.

And I explored another factor that causes enormous dislocations in the global market: advanced countries of the world trading with low-wage countries like China, India, and Vietnam. It is in everyone's interest to see China and India develop as quickly as possible, to alleviate the enormous human suffering and poverty in those countries. But when this development happens at an artificially accelerated rate, through the use of manipulated currency exchange rates, low wages coercively enforced by the government by preventing union formation, and an emphasis on exports to the advanced countries of the world, it can cause real damage to the middle and working classes of the advanced countries of the world. How does the world benefit if India and China develop and the advanced democracies collapse?

Democracy is a fragile thing. One needs only to watch street protests in Greece and Spain to realize that people will not long suffer 20 and 30 percent unemployment rates. They will take action. I can only hope their actions are directed purposefully at the real cause of their problems.

I also discussed why economists just don't get it. Fewer than a handful were able to warn us about the coming economic crisis. Either they don't understand how economics works, or they're being paid by bankers and corporations to hide the truth from us. I don't care which it is. I just wish they'd admit it.

Markets need not be so unpredictable and volatile. If markets are more open and more transparent, and more bankers are arrested for fraud, more information, not less, will be incorporated in securities prices. As more information is incorporated, it will become less likely that there will be new information disruptive enough to cause a boom or a bust.

Obviously you can't have a few very large banks determining asset prices across all markets by how much they're willing to lend people with small down payments. If someone puts up no money to buy an asset like a house, she hasn't really bought the house; the bank has bought the house. And if five overleveraged banks with little shareholder supervision get into a bidding contest for homes in, say, a town like Phoenix, there's no limit to how high prices can go. One bank pays $400,000 for a house or finances a home for that much with no money down, and six months later the bank across town finances the same house for $500,000 and then another bank does so for $600,000. In this world of circular logic, the house ends up being worth $1 million, yet all that has actually happened is that the house has been passed around among a number of banking entities. This is not a market.

I have argued strongly that only an idiot would ever lend money to a sovereign government. I know this sounds counterintuitive, because we grow up thinking that lending to big governments is the safest form of lending there is, and we know a lot of people still haven't learned this lesson because they're still lending to the United States at 2 to 3 percent a year. Trust me. They're about to learn the lesson.

I've also discussed that traditional investments just won't cut it in the future. Financial investments, paper investments, and investments in securities with promises to repay in dollars are not going to work in a world in which the dollar is devaluing greatly. It's already happening. The dollar was off by 29 percent relative to other currencies as of 2011 and was off more than two-thirds relative to the price of gold just since 2008. Stocks, corporate bonds, and government bonds all do poorly as hedges against future unanticipated inflation, and that is the real threat the world faces in the future. As I said, arguing about whether you get 1 percent or 1.1 percent from your five-year CD is silly in a world in which you are repaid in dollars that can purchase 50 percent of what they could back when you invested the monies. If inflation has the ability to eat up 50 percent of your purchasing power, that is the risk you should be dealing with in your investments, not trying to maximize a small difference in real return.

So my recommendation is to invest in hard assets, not financial assets. These real assets do very well as a hedge against unanticipated future inflation, but they don't generate substantial real returns. To generate a real return with your money, you have to take real risk, and in this environment, it makes more sense to just preserve your purchasing power and not try to hit any home runs. There will be more losers than winners in the future. I want to keep you in the winner category.

I described an ideal way to purchase a home using the 30-year, fixed-rate money that is available only to home buyers and gives you a safe perch from which to watch the dollar collapse because of inflation. If it happens in the next three years, you'll make more than ten times on your equity investment in the house. If it happens in the next seven years, you'll make more than five or six times your equity investment. It's hard to imagine losing money on such an asset purchase if you are careful about researching the price you're paying for the home.

I may have buried the lead in this book as I think the most important chapter in this book is the last one (Chapter 13), which describes gold as both a yardstick and an investment. Given gold's recent performance relative to the dollar and to the stock market, people are looking at gold as an investment vehicle, but many have concluded that they have missed out on what they think is the latest bubble. I disagree.

Gold would be properly priced today if somehow the Federal Reserve never printed another dollar. What are the odds of that? You tell me where the government is going to get $1.3 trillion a year to fund its deficit, which is growing with this recession, and the additional trillion-dollar annual loss from Social Security and Medicare that it will be facing in six or seven years. A country that is $14 trillion in debt is not going to be able to borrow forever at 3 percent, especially when that debt is growing at $1 trillion to $2 trillion a year. I don't see the United States defaulting on its debts, but it already is partially defaulting by allowing Bernanke to counterfeit money and pay off government obligations with phony new currency.

In trying to be realistic, I feel obligated to tell my readers things exactly as I see them. Unfortunately, in these troubled times, my books are devoted to pointing out problems with the current system that could lead to even more serious economic problems in the future. I do, however, want to end on an optimistic note by talking about potential solutions.

I believe that almost all of our problems result from a single flaw in our system. I believe that almost all of our economic and banking and education and environmental and health-care problems result from governments of the world being more receptive to corporate and banking ideas than to the will of their people. Our governments, especially in the

United States, have been bought off by the highest bidder. It used to be true that what was good for GM was good for the country. So in the past, if wealthy families and corporations controlled our government, they could at least argue that this would make the country more stable and provide more growth. This is no longer true.

In the new globalized world, jobs move to the countries with the lowest wages. It should be alarming to you that Barack Obama appointed the chief executive officer of General Electric Corporation (GE) as his jobs czar. GE has added 60,000 new jobs over the last ten years. Unfortunately, GE has done this by adding 100,000 jobs overseas and cutting 40,000 jobs in the United States.

The beauty of democracy is not that people think that any individual citizen is smarter than the president. It is that there is strength and knowledge in numbers and groups make better decisions than individuals. Democracy, when it loses this important feedback mechanism, loses its whole raison d'etre. As long as big banks and big corporations can write legislation in Washington, our democracy will suffer, and without proper regulation of the banks, our economy will suffer, too.

So the good news is that these myriad problems can be reduced to one: controlling corporate power in Washington by eliminating lobbyists and making corporate campaign contributions illegal. The bad news, of course, is how difficult this is to do. Think how difficult it's going to be for voters to organize themselves, retake their country from the most powerful banks, the biggest corporations, the entire corrupted Congress, and the presidency of the United States, which have the support of almost all mainstream traditional media. I don't see any way to accomplish this within the system. Many people think that all we need to do is write new laws because they don't realize that the lawmakers are corrupt. Others suggest that we need to vote the bastards out, but with a two-party system in which both are more than corrupt, what difference does it make to vote a Republican out and put a Democrat in? They both take money from banks and corporations in exchange for their votes.

No. The only solution I see is to start a third political party. Given the importance of the issue, and to prevent dissent among Americans, who are easily divided and distracted, I would like to keep the new party simple. Its sole mission should be to remove campaign money from elections, to make elections publicly financed, and to throw all the lobbyists out of Washington. It's a big task, and it is a notion that will be difficult to advance without any corporate or banking money, but I think the American people are ready to get behind such a movement. It would not be enough just to win the presidency. The new third party would have to win a majority of the House and Senate as well.

The stumbling block, of course, is the media. As the candidacies of previous third-party candidates like Ross Perot and

Ralph Nader demonstrated, as soon as they began to get traction and demonstrate that they might control as much as 20 or 25 percent of the vote, the media attacked—not their policies but the candidates themselves. How many of you have now concluded that Ross Perot was crazy or that Ralph Nader was deranged? Nothing could be further from the truth. Everything these men predicted has come true.

Ross Perot was the first to warn us of our blossoming government debt and deficits, and Ralph Nader has spent a lifetime fighting corporate lobbyists and banking lobbyists, yet somehow the public has concluded that both are crazy. I can only tell you that I will consider it a badge of honor if I ever become so famous that the traditional media call me crazy. I certainly like the company.

Once we regain control of our government, we need to take specific action. First, we need to break up the big banks. Everything I've talked about in this book is a result of allowing these big banks to get too large. When a bank is too big to fail, it's too big to operate. There's no way you can break up a $2 trillion bank operating in 140 countries over the weekend if it gets in trouble. It's impossible. And yet, if it were broken into ten smaller banks, I believe the combined stock price of all ten new banks would exceed the stock price of the old big bank. So I think shareholders would actually make money on the breakup. The only loser would be the big bank's CEO, who likes presiding over an empire.

We also have to put strict limits on the amount of leverage that banks can incorporate in their lending. When I first moved to Wall Street in 1981, I found out that banks were leveraged 6:1. I remember how overleveraged I thought that sounded. I knew commercial bankers. I ate dinner with commercial bankers. I went to parties and went dancing with commercial bankers, and I wouldn't have trusted the ability of any of them to lend six dollars and be repaid on five of it. They weren't that smart, they weren't that good, and they weren't that experienced. Yet they had leveraged themselves up to 6:1, which means that if only one dollar out of six went bad, their equity account was wiped out and the bank was bankrupted. I didn't understand how they survived from year to year.

So imagine my surprise today when I see that US banks are leveraged 30:1 and European banks are leveraged 40:1. Now the same commercial bankers I knew back in 1981 can lose only one dollar for every $40 they lend and they wipe out their bank. In today's world, we know that means not that their creditors absorb any additional losses but that the government steps in, bails the bank out, and makes the taxpayer pay for the bank's mistakes.

Of course in the modern world, bank leverage is not limited just to debt on its balance sheet. It makes no sense to limit bank leverage without looking at a bank's derivatives positions, and when you examine its derivatives, you cannot look just at net positions but at its gross positions and exposures.

JPMorgan reports hundreds of billions of dollars of net derivative positions on its balance sheet in its annual financial statement and yet has tens of trillions of dollars of gross derivative positions. The problem with looking only at net positions is that in a crisis there is no assurance that your counterparty will survive to pay you off. As a matter of fact, it's likely in a crisis that you will owe money on all the bad sides of your transactions, while all the trades that are good for you but cost your counterparties money may lead to their insolvency and their inability to pay you. Hedging a trillion-dollar position means nothing if you cannot ensure that your counterparty will survive a crisis. In essence you've created a perfect hedge, perfect that is in that it will always fail in a crisis, as your counterparties who have losses themselves will fail to pay you.

Of course you know my position on the credit default swap (CDS) market. It needs to close. We cannot have a system in which all the boats at sea are linked by enormous iron chains (CDSs) and are insuring each other against sinking. When one goes, they all go. Capitalism cannot exist if poorly managed, misguided firms are not allowed to fail. Creative destruction is one of the great strengths of capitalism, whereas the state enterprises of more socialist countries survive for decades regardless of how little value they bring to society.

We must also address, in this brave new world, the question of what we do with trade with low-wage countries such as China and India. It doesn't make any sense to make healthy, growing democracies out of China and India if doing so threatens the advanced economic democracies of the world. The reason the world holds up Europe and the United States as economic miracles is that the more freedom and liberty you give your citizens, the more economic choices they have. And the more they control their own economic and political lives, the more developed the country, the greater the growth, and the greater the prosperity. Until we return some manufacturing and low-skill jobs to the United States, we will have a permanent class of unemployed here, fostering economic and political instability.

Maybe our brave new world doesn't stop just with reforms of the banking system. Maybe once we regain control of our own governments and eliminate the excessive power of special interests like banks and corporations, we'll find a different world than that driven by corporate greed and corporate motivations to maximize profits. Maybe in this brave new world, people will be less interested in consumption and materialism as the only goals in life. What would a society look like that was organized more toward maximizing individuals' goals and aspirations than corporate profits? Certainly there would be less growth for growth's sake. Growth in the long term does provide job opportunities, but the primary beneficiaries of growth are corporations, which see their earnings multiply and their stock prices increase. In a new world that recognizes that natural resources are not limitless and population growth must be constrained, we have to examine not only how to create sustainable growth but how to motivate a capitalist system to perform in a no-growth environment.

There is good growth and bad growth. Good growth results from new ideas about how to better use resources and create better and more useful products and services. Wasteful growth results from nothing more than a bigger population that is seeking more and more material goods. It doesn't necessarily benefit anyone especially because humans are more interested in relative wealth than absolute wealth. I know people with four cars and three boats and three homes who are enormously depressed because their next-door neighbors have bigger homes and faster boats.

So what will this brave new world look like if it doesn't emphasize corporate profits, consumption, and materialism? What is it that people really want in today's world? If people can learn to break free of the false measures of success placed on them by their corporate-dominated culture, I think they will quickly come to realize that more and bigger houses and boats and cars are not what life is about. I think many 65-year-olds who pursued careers at big corporations for 40 years become enormously depressed when they realize that they didn't pursue their real passions in life and sold out for the almighty buck. If only we would give older people more of a voice, perhaps they would give us a hint of the right direction to take our lives.

I know I'm biased as an author, but I think this brave new world is going to consist of creative entrepreneurial individuals who are creating not only new products and new services to sell in a capitalist environment but also more music and more books and better communication and more ways for Americans and other peoples of the world to meet with families and friends in communities that are supportive of communal work and communal enjoyment.

I don't know when it became the rule that people have to work 40 to 60 hours a week and carry cell phones so they can be in contact with their offices 20 hours a day. We're supposed to be a rich country. Why wouldn't it make sense for us to work less and have more leisure time?

But, more important, we need to make the fundamental decision early on in our lives that we will pursue work that we find enjoyable. We need to get away from career decisions based on unmanageable student debt or newly acquired housing debt that forces us into making money today at the cost of giving up our life's aspirations and goals. We need to get back to our roots and live Franklinesque lives of invention, creativity, poetry, music, literature, and enjoying the companionship of others. What a wonderful world it could be.

INDEX

ABOUT THE AUTHOR

John R. Talbott is the bestselling author of nine books on economics and politics, including *The Coming Crash in the Housing Market* (2003), *Where America Went Wrong*, 2006's *Sell Now!: The End of the Housing Bubble* (2004) and *Contagion: The Financial Epidemic That Is Sweeping the Global Economy* (2008), which predicted that the subprime mortgage problem developing in the United States would infect not only prime mortgages, but the stock market, the commercial real estate market, and the municipal bond market, threatening the solvency of banks and governments around the globe and leading to a long and painful recession. Finally, *The 86 Biggest Lies on Wall Street* (2009) exposed the ineptness of the government's response to the crisis and the futility of enacting real reform of Wall Street.

Formerly an investment banker for Goldman Sachs and a Visiting Scholar at UCLA's Anderson School of Management, Talbott has written peer-reviewed academic research on democracy, inequality, AIDS prevention, and developing country economics and has acted as an economic adviser to Jordan and Russia. He has made presentations on economics and politics throughout the United States and in Italy and Australia. He graduated from Cornell's School of Engineering and received an MBA from UCLA. His work has appeared in the *Wall Street Journal, Financial Times, Boston Globe, San Francisco Chronicle, Herald Tribune, New Republic, The Huffington Post,* and *Salon.* He has appeared as a financial expert on television for CNN, CBS, Fox News, CNBC, FBN, CSPAN and MSNBC as well as on hundreds of radio programs.

John offers financial consulting advice to individuals and families on a very personal and confidential basis. You can learn more about his One on One consulting activities at www.StopTheLying.com